I'd Rather be Shelling on Niue!

Betty Kilgour

Detselig Enterprises Limited
Calgary, Alberta

Betty Kilgour

Three Hills, Alberta

Canadian Cataloguing in Publication Data

Kilgour, Betty.
    I'd rather be shelling on Niue!

ISBN 0-920490-76-X

    1. Kilgour, Betty – Anecdotes. 2. Niue –
Biography – Anecdotes, facetiae, satire, etc.
3. Niue – Description and travel.   I. Title.
DU430.N5K54 1988   996'.1   C88-091197-2

© 1988 by Detselig Enterprises Limited
P.O. Box G 399
Calgary, Alberta T3A 2G3

Printed in Canada   SAN 115-0324   ISBN 0-920490-76-X

This book is dedicated to our grandchildren:

Chelsea and Cheyenne Price,
Dallas, Page, Tyrel and Brandy Kilgour
Nathan Anderson
Andrew, Marcie, Robbie and Chuck Parry.

With much love.

My private dream is one day you will write a book and dedicate it to me!

Contents

Cover picture and book illustrations by Ben Crane

Foreword

Most people have never heard of Niue. Even people who know the South Pacific quite well, as New Zealanders feel they do, frequently confuse Niue with Nauru: "Niue. That's the place where the phosphate comes from, isn't it?"

It isn't. Nauru is the phosphate island.

Niue lays claim to being the smallest self-governing population in the world. There are less than 2,500 people but a sovereign entity, surrounded by clear blue ocean, hundreds of miles from its nearest neighbours (Tonga and Samoa). Niue is perhaps best remembered by outsiders for the hospitality extended to visitors.

Hospitality and courtesy may serve as a shield against strangers, for Niue is small and vulnerable. Most visitors stay no longer than a few days, some maybe for a week or two. They leave knowing little more than their hosts would have wished.

Betty and Bill Kilgour stayed longer and learned more. They learned a lot about the people living on Niue – Niueans and expatriates like themselves. What they learned shines through the pages of this book. Kindness met kindness. Betty responded generously to the Niueans' warm welcome. This enabled the Kilgours, little by little, to go beyond the superficial courtesies that are rather often the limit of contact between people of different cultures.

There is a happy truthfulness about Betty's story. She portrays a rich tapestry of human strengths and weaknesses, seeing and writing about others as she does about herself, with refreshing candour.

We New Zealanders who were living on Niue took the Kilgours to our hearts. Not the least of the Kilgours' admired characteristics were their warmth, their quiet humour, and the twinkle in their eye. Maybe we like to think of Canadians with a good measure of Scottish or Irish blood in their veins, as little different from ourselves; New Zealanders accept Canadians quickly; there are probably no people on earth whom we could have better reason to trust.

Many long term visitors to Niue who read these pages will think: "This could have been my book, if only I could write as Betty does, if I had her insight, if I could have had the enterprise and initiative to do what she did. . . ."

Thank you Betty Kilgour, for enriching the memories of all who have stayed on Niue for long enough to get to know the Island and it's people.

Malcolm McNamara
New Zealand Representative on Niue
1982 - 1984

Acknowledgments

This book would never have reached its fruition without the help of many:

Cathy Saxby, my delightful editor for her practiced eye and constant support.

May Misfeldt for her own individual help and kindness.

Ted Giles for (Glory Be!) taking another chance with me and my material!

Ben Crane for his excellent art work.

Dr. Malcolm McNamara for providing the Foreword and Jane McNamara for providing facts and figures.

Jim Butler for providing his marvelous photos and expertise.

Pete Cote for spending hours proofreading.

Lower Hutt Alona for refreshing my memory in regards to Island customs.

Sir Robert Rex and the people of Niue – thank you for your acceptence and love while we were stationed on your beautiful island.

Last, but certainly not least – my love and thanks to Bill, my strength, my critic, my best friend.

Detselig Enterprises Ltd. appreciates the financial
assistance for its 1988 publishing program from

Alberta Foundation for the Literary Arts
Canada Council
Department of Communications
Alberta Culture

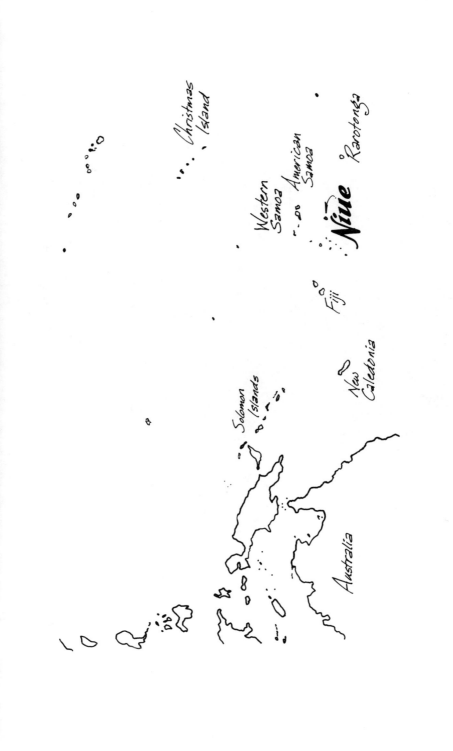

The Flame Burns On

There are times, especially when the winter winds blow cold from the north and the days are short, that I wish fervently I were back shelling on Niue.

Through countless centuries people of all kinds have tried to figure out what it is that burns within the human heart to lure them away from hearth and home on yet, another great adventure. It is a fire so strong it can only be appeased by travelling to all sorts of remote corners of the earth, many times uncomfortable and the odd time even dangerous. Whatever causes this phenomenon, both Bill and I are infected and I can assure you it burns hotter and brighter with each passing year and with each adventure.

We had been home from our two-year-stint with CUSO in Tanzania (So This Is Africa!) only a couple of years when the fire started flaring once more. Any program on other corners of the world held us spellbound. On hearing of some lucky soul going abroad, even as far as Mexico, we started drooling. Bill, however had to get our farming operation straightened out and I had to get to know my children and they me: we were settling in like two sane sedentary people. Despite this, and having launched two daughters on the marriage road, the flame was burning.

I started complaining, which was not a new thing for me, about never getting away: "Everyone goes on holidays but us! These cows get off this place more often than I do!"

"God Bets, I took you to Africa for two years! What do you want for pity's sake!"

1

I didn't know what I wanted – so I attacked the garden, the house, everything with moronic fervor hoping to quell the urge.

The self-righteous me, decided Bill was working too hard on the farm. I simply must get him away. The only one I fooled was myself I'm sure. I searched every paper, listened to every word on the radio looking for that wonderful opening. I'd preserve the life of my husband by dragging him off to some godforsaken place with the possibility of there not being enough to eat! Logic was not part of my thinking you see.

One day I was scrubbing my kitchen floor half-listening to CBC radio when I heard a blurb about WUSC recruiting UN volunteers. WUSC didn't mean a thing to me, it sounded like a laundry detergent – but UN did, as did volunteers. I upset the bucket of water in my hurry to write it all down. But having missed the address, I peeked outside to see if Bill was about – nary a sign. It was safe to phone the radio station. I didn't stop to figure out, *why* – if it was all to help preserve Bill why did I sneak about. Again, it was not one of my more lucid moments.

Anyway, I got the address of WUSC (World University Services Canada) and wrote an impassioned letter about our wish to help our fellow man and to send us an application form. Funny how my zeal shifted from preserving Bill to saving the rest of the world!

I didn't breath a word of this to anyone – just went about with dreams of other places going round and round in my head. And just about broke my neck getting to town to the Post Office before Bill. I'm not sure why I did that when I would have to show him the application sometime.

Finally, they came. Glory be – they looked marvelous! I made a very special supper, sprayed on my sexiest perfume and went to work on Bill.

I reported what I had heard, leaning very much toward how I was not wanting to bother him – being as how he was working himself to death on the farm. But Bill had lived with me long enough to know me well.

"Bets, what are you going on about?"

So I handed the forms over and by the time we had read them over and we had discussed all the pros and cons, we thought we'd fill out the forms – "there probably won't be any available postings anyway!"

Of course we had to line-up three people to sign for each of us stating all our fine points and not mentioning the "not so fine" ones.

Any posting takes time – there's paper work galore and waiting periods so we just mailed everything off and went on with our lives.

Then one evening we had a phone call from Ottawa. Could, we meet them in Calgary for an interview? "Of Course!" Well, at that time of year I was feeling so housebound I'd have gladly gone twenty miles west to watch the strippers. Another hurdle was over – the waiting.

They hadn't asked us if we wished a particular area or continent so we didn't have a clue where we might end up.

One day, months later, the mails brought a notice – the FAO (Food and Agricultural Organization) of the UN needed a ranch manager for a cattle operation on a small island in the South Pacific. Would we be interested? There was little information on the island itself. It was a coral island south of Samoa, had good weather, and grew passion fruit and limes for export. The cattle operation was amongest the coconut trees.

I don't know about you, but when I'm confronted with little information my imagination takes over. Many times great flights of fancy filled in the empty spots, so you can imagine the picture I drew in my mind of Niue. Bill, meanwhile, had caught my virus and was all gung ho so we hustled off a big "Yes we'd love to."

By the time the FAO had okayed it and their representative on Niue had okayed it, it was late summer 1982 and we were looking harvest in the eye. After a few hurried calls we were given time to take our crop off before leaving. In the meantime, I had the packing to contend with. I had all the cupboards to empty, and dishes, books and furniture to pack away. My daughters arrived to help and we packed, stored and burned. I came away with the impression that you should move every ten years to clean house of accumulations.

But it was all accomplished and early November saw us at the Calgary International Airport bidding a tearful farewell to our kids once more. To top it off a blizzard blew in and when everyone was on board the undercarriage of our plane went out. Bill was telling all and sundry that it happened the moment that Bets' luggage was tossed in! Anyway, they fed us and then herded us off and on to yet another plane for the short trip to Vancouver where the flight to Hawaii was awaiting us.

When travelling you are either dressed wrong for departing or for arriving. It was bitterly cold when we left Calgary and I was in a pure wool suit and high dress boots – very stylish for Calgary, but Hawaii? I just about expired. My boots had rubbed blisters on my heels and even with my jacket off I dripped with sweat. Finally, I dug into one suitcase for some sandals and slipped off my pantihose. I had worn a very sheer blouse – for its perfect collar. It, however, left no doubt as to the colour of my bra, but I couldn't have cared if I was bare under it I was *not* putting on that wool jacket again!

The stopover night was nice, and we were rested by morning and in appropriate clothes. I felt great.

We were at the airport early for our flight as we both love airports. There we met a middle aged divorcee. She was well-dressed, although not too comfortably, in a navy and white suit, high heels and pantihose. By then I was centuries wiser and was wearing a loose shirt, pants, and sandals so I could afford to be critical.

We sat visiting and drinking juice while she told us what a well-seasoned traveller she was. She didn't believe in hitting all the tourist traps, preferring the common people and their mode of living. She had been many wonderful places and was very travel wise. She really impressed me, "Gee wouldn't it be great to be that wealthy, clever and able to handle all sorts of situations!"

The flight to our destination of Western Samoa, was long (about nine hours) but the plane was comfortable and not too full. Every once in a while I'd panic thinking "two years is a long time to be away from my kids" But I managed to calm myself, knowing how quickly the months zip by if your surroundings are new, interesting, and you keep yourself busy.

We also met a couple on the plane enroute to New Guinea to visit their son. Of course Bill with great gusto told the story of how Bets' luggage caused the demise of the first plane we boarded – but the lady (bless her) thought we should watch the undercarriage of this one as she even had a crowbar in her luggage!

Hours later we spotted our first land. What a sight it was. It's impossible to describe the lush green of Samoa or its landscape. It was magnificent. Part deep green vegetation and high hills set in azure seas – this exalted impression was possibly due to my recent departure from late fall Alberta landscape but even today I can still see this beautiful scene.

We landed in Pago Pago (pronounced Pango Pango) in American Samoa and immediately took a tiny plane over to Apia, in Western Samoa. After the luxury of the larger plane this plane was ridiculous – a little ten seater with crates here and there, it looked like it was held together with bandaids. Bill asked the pilot if he started it with a rubberband, but the pilot got even. We hit an air pocket and dropped what felt like 500 feet, boxes and passengers were thrown every which way. Of course the pilot apologized, but I detected a gleam in his eye when he looked at Bill.

When we went to claim our baggage we were told it would be over on the next flight. The pilot couldn't carry the passengers and luggage at the same time. I caught Bill's eye with a look saying, "Don't you *dare* mention my luggage once more." He had seen that look before and knew to be quiet.

This didn't surprise us though as this was our second posting and we were out of our cushy Western world cocoon.

We walked about enjoying the lovely evening. The warm tropical breezes rustled the leaves of the Palms as the Mamas sat in their Mu Mus on the outside benches discussing the day's affairs. There was a little outdoor counter where you could purchase a Coke. I felt the mad rush of our society slowly ease away.

But all was not going well for our seasoned travelling lady. She was storming about complaining of the laxness of the airport, the hotel which was to have a driver there to meet her and everything else she could think of. "Don't you know I'm a tourist?!" she roared. Of course she was, what else could she be making that much noise. A real traveller never gets that excited. My, I was disappointed in her but I know landing in a tropical country in high heels, pantihose and polyester does something to your disposition not to mention your body.

A young Chinese woman, who had introduced herself on the plane as a fellow volunteer also bound for Niue, asked me to accompany her the bathroom. It was typical; messy and chipped but she was horrified. I began to wonder if there was something wrong with me! But then I remembered I had been down this road before and was used to the public washrooms of foreign countries. I told her to be thankful it wasn't just a hole in the ground with a tin shelter around it. I felt quite smug as I consoled her. What a difference experience makes!

Romantic Bubbles

We cleared customs and were taken via taxi into Apia, the capital. We were thrilled we would be in Western Samoa a week. American Samoa is very much influenced by the United States and tourism whereas, Western Samoa is still holding to its own culture.

As we sped along the tree lined road I saw my first *fales* or homes. I had read of these homes. All they consist of is the frame and the roof and floor. The walls are woven from grasses and leaves and tied to the frame. These are kept rolled up, and let down if a storm blows or its a bit cold. The odd house had a bed but everyone seemed to prefer the mats on the floor.

By the time we arrived at our hotel it was nearly 11:00 p.m. and the manager had to be ousted out of bed.

Soon we were in our room and believe me it seemed like we had been on the road longer than two days! We had slipped into a completely different and unique lifestyle.

We reported to the UN headquarters the morning after we arrived.

Bill and I were introduced to everyone, each one out doing the other in officiousness. Once they figured I was sane, sensible and not too much of a hellraiser I was permitted to leave. After all Bill was the official volunteer although *I* know the volunteer's partner is equally important.

I left Bill at the offices, deep in conversation discussing great and wondrous plans for Niue and our future life there.

About a block from our hotel, which was situated on a

point with the majestic Pacific Ocean at its doorsteps, was an open air market.

I have a thing about markets. I'm drawn to them like a pin to a magnet. No matter what country they're in, what size or what they sell. Even if its only wilted lettuce and charcoal. I wander through in a daze. But it isn't the goods for sale that wills me in – I often spend half a day in a market and buy absolutely nothing (much to the disgruntlement of the merchants). No, what I like is free. Its the atmosphere, the smells, the sounds, the sights all blended in a splendid mosaic. I've come to believe I'm a market place junky, absolutely and impossibly addicted to them.

This market was wonderous. It covered a good half city block and sold everything from eight-inch string beans to charcoal. There were vegetables and fruits I had never seen or imagined, fish of all kinds fresh from the ocean, wonderful woven baskets, mats, and purses made right there by ladies sitting crosslegged on mats and, of course, the neat plastic stuff which is part and parcel of all markets.

So you can well imagine I spent a good deal of my time wandering starry eyed through the market.

But I also shot through all the other little stores as well as the big Burns Philp (known simply as 'BP' to the locals), the chain store of the Pacific. I had read so much about this store and had built it up to such impossible heights of fancy I was bound to be disappointed. The exterior was as I had imagined, dignified but weather beaten, sitting solidly on the alien soil like a remittance man with little left but his aristocratic breeding. But the inside was disappointing to the extreme. I expected to see an old decrepit sailor with bare feet and dirty white dungarees rolled up to his bony knees, his eyes bloodshot and chin covered in a great grey beard; but all I saw was one native Mama looking at the polyester fabric and a bored clerk lazily picking away at her purple nailpolish. Where were the characters of Somerset Maugham and James Michener? The dusty shelves were nearly empty, as empty as my heart when my romantic bubble burst.

But my faith was restored as I rounded the corner by the Post Office and literally ran into a Samoan policeman. Now there was something to gaze upon! A huge fellow in the traditional uniform; helmet, brass buttoned jacket and lava lava which came to his hairy knees. Heavy wool socks and shoes which had to have come from the "British Boot Shop" covered his size fourteen feet.I quelled the urge to walk round and round him sighing, but I moved across the street instead. There I could view this wonderous being in relative privacy.

I wandered past Aggie Greys, the hotel for the elite – the moneyed tourists. Aggie Grey, the owner, started out during World War II with a portable hamburger stand; walking miles to sell her hamburgers. She became very well-known and was shrewd enough to build first a small guesthouse, then expand to the deluxe hotel it is today. Much of the timber used to build the hotel was brought in by Navy ships, as she had many important connections in the military. Aggie Grey, now a very old lady, is still in charge and greets many a guest with a large whiskey and soda on the house.

The weather was humid to the extreme, a lot like the coastal area of Tanzania. It was the start of the rainy season and sudden tropical storms could catch you in a second. Within five minutes the streets would be under six or more inches of water. I would dodge into a building at the first rain drop. If you couldn't get to shelter in time you would be absolutely drenched but it was a lovely warm rain and once the hot sun came out you'd dry in a few minutes.

I finally bought an umbrella – my very first as there is little need for umbrellas on an Alberta farm. I felt quite ridiculous carrying the thing. It brought to mind the dapper gentlemen in England I had seen carrying umbrellas and I tried to swing it likewise, but I found I was clunking too many people on the kneecaps so I just stuck it under my arm.

The few days on Samoa were up quickly and we found ourselves on the plane bound for Niue and more adventures.

A Little History

The name 'Niue' is composed of 'Niu' – a coconut tree and 'E' – behold. In the old Niuean legend it is said that the first discoverers found no coconut trees on the island, which is very likely. A young man from the island visited one of the Tongan islands and sought the hand of a maiden of high rank. Her father did not favour this marriage, particularly when he heard there were no coconut trees on that island. He gave the young suitor two seed nuts with instructions to go home and plant them and when they were producing to come back for the girl. The young man took the nuts and *also* eloped with the girl. On stepping ashore he called out – Niu E or as we would put it – Hey look you guys, Coconuts!

Niue is believed to have been inhabited for over a thousand years; some authorities believe there were two principal migrations to the island; one from Samoa and one from Tonga, with some contacts with Aitutaki and Rarotonga. There is also a Fijian influence. Over the years Niueans have developed their own unique lifestyle and language.

On June 20, 1744, the Niueans spotted Captain James Cook's ship, the "Resolution" on the horizon. The following day Captain Cook made three attempts to go ashore and received such a hostile welcome at each point he was forced to give up. On one attempt a sailor was hit in the chest by a spear and stones were thrown from the cliffs. Cook wrote in his diary, "we were accousted with the ferocity of wild boars!" and named it *Savage Island*, a name which the island had for many years.

The Niueans had a tradition of fierce challenge to any

stranger. Niue, being so isolated and vulnerable, had a far larger amount of distrust than some of the other islands. Niuean history states that a Niuean painted his teeth with the blood red dye of the hula banana and greeted Cook with a war dance. On seeing the blood red teeth, Cook figured they were being attacked by cannibals. The Niuean believe that all Cook experienced was a good healthy challenge which he mistook for outright aggression, giving the island the unfortunate name it was to be known by for the next century.

Missionaries had already penetrated other surrounding islands and the London Mission Society was busy evangelizing them. John Williams, a well-known missionary, was determined to land missionaries on every inhabited island. However, on attempting to land on Niue with two preachers and their wives he was met with the same hostile reception as Cook. It seemed quite hopeless. Thinking it over Williams decided he would have to capture two young Niuean boys, raise them and send them back to teach their own. This he accomplished but I'm sure this very action turned the natives against whites for a very long time.

This action was coupled with a great deal of slave trading that was going on in the Pacific. The traders were sending the slaves to work the cotton fields of Australia, Tahiti and Fiji.

The Peruvian slave traders were dreaded. At times capturing one hundred or more slaves at one strike to work the guano deposits (a valuable fertilizer which the Europeans bought in great quantities) in Chili. At one time there were more than fifty vessels "black birding" as the slave trade was called.

One of the most vile traders was an American dubbed "Bully Hayes." He was cruel and brutal to the extreme. If there was a particularly hostile island he would send two or three natives who were infected with measles ashore to infect the people. This disease was deadly and soon what Islanders were left were subdued.

In time the two young men raised by the mission were brought home to Niue and set there in 1840. They started spreading Christianity to all, but there was still a lot of suspicion and fear of European influence and disease. The men were accepted, however. In time other missionaries and Europeans were welcome. European dress was, to a small extent, adopted and the older ladies still favour the Mother Hubbard gowns and big white hats assumed appropriate by the missionaries.

As a result of several requests to the British Government by Niuean leaders, supported by missionaries and traders, a British protectorate was declared over the island in 1900. In June 1901 control of Niue was bequeathed to New Zealand and was incorporated into New Zealand territory.

Niue was originally annexed and administered as part of the Cook Islands. Niue, however, had neither historic nor cultural ties with the Cooks and wanted to preserve its own identity, thus a separate administration was established in 1904. This comprised of the post of a Resident Commissioner who had wide political, judicial and administrative powers, and an Island Council which played an advisory role.

This pattern of administration lasted for over fifty years. In time the Resident Commissioner passed on some of his powers to the Niueans and from 1960 on the Niuean people began to accept the fact that Niue should work towards a greater degree of autonomy leading to some form of self-government.

The new Niue Constitution came into effect October 1974 and the island became self-governing with a free association with New Zealand; that is, Niueans are British subjects but citizens of New Zealand.

The executive functions of government are carried out by the Premier, Sir Robert Rex, and three other members of the Assembly. The Niue Assembly consists of twenty members and a speaker.

The Niuean ladies, being Polynesian, are golden skinned with either long black wavy or fuzzy hair. The young are lively and slender but as they age they tend to fatten. A lot of them wear western dress now but when it's very hot or for working they use the pareau and lava lavas which island people have worn for years. There are always brilliant prints, lots with Island flowers and designs. I found ninety percent spoke English although at first they were shy and would just look at me strangely. Interestingly, I found I would start speaking the Swahili I thought I never learned during my adventures in Africa.

Niuean lady and daughter with passion fruit.

The ladies are very industrious, working hard in their homes and bush gardens. Most of the work is basic with little modern equipment to help. But when the work is done they always have their weaving and embroidery work at hand to do. The Niuean weaving is of very high quality and is taught to girls at a very young age. When the weather is dry, the ladies gather in the damp caves to weave. Baskets of all types and sizes, mats for the floor, hats wonderfully decorated and all sorts of other weaving is done by village women and bought for very little to be re-sold in the craft store in Alofi. There is little export though the quality is high it can not be mass produced due to the small population.

The women's embroidery work is very colourful, usually

tropical flowers done in the satin stitch. Pillow cases are a great favourite. The whole top will be covered by the pattern and usually a frill of the same material is sewn all around.

Some of the village women were hired to pollinate the passion fruit when the blossoms were ready. The Agricultural Department had tried using bees for this but it didn't work so women were hired; they were trustworthy and the government knew they'd be thorough. Other women worked in town, at Central Office, the Hospital, or held other positions but most women stayed busy with their gardens, children and home like they have for centuries.

The Niuean men were also golden skinned and with their dark hair and black eyes were a handsome lot. The men in times past were the hunters and the fishermen providing meat for their family and it's still like that but now many work for the government for Public Works or farm labourers. The only thing I noticed, they still feel their job is to hunt and fish and as long as they show up for work it's not too important to actually lather up a great sweat! Of course there are many exceptions and some of my friends were good hard workers. And all of them were extremely likeable.

Niuean man.

All Niuean children receive primary education in government schools. There are grade schools in nearly every village and each had their own particular school uniform. The boys usually wore white shirts and shorts and the girls various coloured tunics, sometimes with blouses under and sometimes not. All the teachers with village schools were Niuean, having taken their training in New Zealand or at the University of the South Pacific – Fiji.

If the children go on to High School they are bussed into Alofi where there are not only Niuean teachers but also many from New Zealand. English is gradually replacing Niuean in schools and is being taught at an early age. The standard of education is based on the New Zealand curriculum.

The lifestyle is laid back and easy, as in most tropical countries and I can understand this. In the very hot season there is no way a person, no matter how industrious can rush about. One story that I heard, whether true or not I don't know. It seems some missionaries on the island in the 1800s decided, after they made all converts wear hot western style clothes, they'd also make them industrious. They decided they would have all the breadfruit, banana and coconut trees chopped down then the natives would have to hoe gardens and work for their food! I'm very thankful the Niueans were a lot smarter then the missionaries and didn't comply.

The Niueans were very patriotic, in fact a platoon of 150 Niuean soldiers fought in the First World War. Some fought in Eygpt and were later sent to France where the cold which they were not used to coming from a tropical island, caused much sickness and death with few coming home, a disaster to Niue with its small population. When World War II reared its dark face over the world Niue decided not send a regular platoon because of the loss of so many men in the First War but many Niuean men went to New Zealand to enlist on their own.

We Arrive and Settle

As our plane circled and descended over the water it looked several shades of blue and aquamarine. Bill practically had to hold my feet I was trying so hard to see everything. The land looked so green and lush, with neat rows of some kind of vine, but before I could figure out what they were, we were taxing to a stop.

A view of Niue Island from the air.

The airport seemed so tiny with a little fenced off part absolutely packed with people waving! Heavens, I thought, who's on the plane worth that welcome! I soon found out everyone met every plane, it was something to do.

The young people from Central Office, where Doris was to

work, had gone all out and had a great banner with "Welcome Doris" waving. We were through baggage and customs in no time and found ourselves greeted with leis and welcomes. Mr. Z and his wife, were there to greet us. Mr. Z was head of the UN on the island and was to be Bill's boss. His wife was very blond, very English and very proper.

Soon we were in a little car heading for the hotel where, we were told, we'd stay until our house was prepared. That was fine by me, I was absolutely pooped from preparations for our departure, tearful farewells and my too active imagination causing sleepless nights.

We travelled so fast and were so crammed in the car I couldn't see a thing but upon stepping out at the hotel I just gasped. The ocean was right there, so calm and beautiful, with palm trees waving in the breeze. It was a tropical paradise.

After small talk and a cool drink we were left to settle, that is, settle as much as you can in a corner of heaven!

Each morning Bill would go to the office and I'd lounge about eating, sleeping and writing our kids back home. The hotel was situated about two miles from the main town but I'd stroll down each day for something to do or I'd visit with the hotel cook, the waitresses and laundresses. There would often be people from other islands or New Zealand on Niue on business. A judge from New Zealand, a Negro American teacher from the University of the South Pacific – Fiji, and radio ham operators from the U.S. to mention but a few. Other white people stationed on Niue would pop into the hotel just for a visit so I quickly learned what to expect from Niueans and other Polagis (whites) as well as what our lifestyle might be like.

While still at the hotel Bill decided I would need a vehicle to get around. Our future house was two and a half miles from downtown and the villages were all around the island. He knew I'd want to tour about visiting.

Vehicles on Niue are few and far between and especially used ones for sale. Most all are very rusty and battered due to the climate, plus very expensive. We started asking around.

There was one old car for sale but the owner was asking $2,000 New Zealand. I didn't tell him I'd seen better in a demolition derby! I was still in a romantic fog. But Bill thought if we let him think we weren't interested he'd possibly lower the price. Ha! What we didn't know then was there was a shortage of cars. No one ever put their price down. A day later it was picked up by a man from New Zealand for $2,500. Now we were stuck. But there, as on all small islands, was a very good coconut telegraph which would pass information from one end to the other: "Some strange new Polagis were at the hotel and wanted a vehicle."

Bill came home one afternoon with the news, "I met a Niuean fellow Bets, a minister, and he's trying to sell a vehicle for a couple who left the island. Let's go have a look." Our spirits rose and off we went. It was a jeep without a top and to get in you crawled over the edge! I just loved it! I could see myself tearing around the island, on errands of mercy – or something. This before I even tried to start the thing. Bill, however, had different visions, like me flying out of the thing when I hit a palm tree or getting caught in rain storms. We were back to square one.

But that evening who walked into the hotel but the Police Chief himself looking for Bill. I panicked for a moment – what had we done now! But he was there to sell us a car! The story was, he had an extra one he'd let us have cheap: "Very good condition, very reliable, just the right size for your wife, Bill." After losing out on the first car Bill glanced out the window at it and said "We'll take it" all in five seconds flat.

But when I saw it I just had to laugh. My wheelbarrow was bigger than it was! A tiny, green Morris Minor. I sat in it and it was like sitting on a kid's sleigh. Bill lifted up the hood and the battery was smaller than the one in the lawn mower. But we turned it on and it started. We paid $1,500 which was atrocious. It was held together with rust but we figured if you can't trust the Police Chief who can you trust. It probably wouldn't go very fast but still I had visions of terrifying the island and chasing little old ladies up the Post Office steps.

My trusty little car which carried me many wonderful miles.

Next was our future home. I knew we were to live in a little house in Fualahi – just beside the airport. It was a tiny village of about twelve to fourteen houses in a semicircle with a green (lawn) in the centre. These houses were all of the same design and made for the the whites on Niue who were there usually for two year terms. The house was constructed of cement blocks and an iron roof. Most of the homes on the island were built the same way after the hurricane *Ofa* swept many away. What we didn't know was, the house designated for us was already occupied by an Irishman who was teaching at Niue High School. The very last thing we wanted was someone else's house. There were apartments empty elsewhere! But Mr. Z, being what he was, an Englishman who hadn't yet learned there are places far more wonderful than London, and people far superior to Englishmen, wanted "that Irish bum out of his area!" Of course he was Bill's boss and I knew to be careful but I also have a fair share of Irish blood in my veins and it took a great deal to keep it under control.

Bill and I met Jim, our Irishman, and tried to explain we didn't need nor want his home. But Jim understood the situation and didn't hold it against us. and moved to an apartment. Soon the painters were in (something that wasn't done for Jim) and the house started to look bright and new. Our home was on the end of the green and was much smaller than the others, but we didn't mind. It was certainly big enough for us.

We were each given a survival kit which contained the very basics: pots, electric fry pan, dishes, cutlery, towels and sheets to use until we had our own. I shopped for spices and all the little things you need but take for granted at home. After measuring all the windows and the day bed I bought yards of fabric to cover them, as well as cotton to make sheets. It was truly setting up housekeeping from scratch. We had shipped a trunk from Canada with a few extras but it didn't arrive for some time.

Each day I'd drive up and see how my house was coming along and wait with anticipation for the big day. We were at the hotel for a month. While there several families became friends. One couple, Gail and Brian Gillespie, and their boys Steven and David, visited everyday they came to town. I'm not sure exactly what the boys thought but when another friend was preparing to leave the island and told Gail they were moving to the hotel for the last three days as all their belongings were packed. One of the boys piped up "Well, I hope you asked Betty for permission!" I guess we had been there so long the boys figured we owned it.

We finally moved into our new home just before Christmas. I had gotten to know many of the Polagis in Fualahi and liked them. One girl, Leigh, was a seamstress and helpful; a great combination. She sewed my curtains and soon the little house was looking cozy, not elegant or modern, but cozy.

I found the odd pretty picture in old magazines and stuck them on the walls, picked wild flowers and arranged the furniture.

I know the house would have given some people claustrophobia it was so small. I felt like I was living in a group of closets. The kitchen had only about a three-foot-width working area between the cupboards and I could stand in the centre, and reach out and almost touch the walls.

Niue has quite a good electrical power system and each

staff house has a small fridge and electric stove. There was cold running water, a toilet, a very small shower and sink, and very small and primitive heater – a little square box about two feet high and wide with a small fire box. Each morning I'd start the thing up with scrap of paper and kindling adding the wood as I went. I grew up chopping wood and starting old time coal stoves so it was no big deal. If I kept it burning hard I could heat the water for the day in a half-hour. (I later found dried coconut husks burned well and slowly and if I wanted a fast blaze the pods of the flame tree were great.) I must brag though – I and one island friend were the only women in the settlement who could run the stove. The men had that chore to look forward to in the other homes!

There were three tiny bedrooms. One of these I used as a store room for the deep freeze and later a sewing machine. The front room had linoleum on the floor which was great. All the other floors were cement, but on these I tossed Niuean mats which helped cushion the feet. It took two months for my ankles to handle the hard floors.

The furniture was basic; single cots, table, chairs and wicker easy chairs. Also a day bed – a cot with drawers under and a foam pad on top. If you sat with your back against the wall your feet wouldn't touch the floor, if your feet touched the floor your back ached, if you lay on it your bones hurt. I used it to throw my junk on.

The windows were huge with many individual adjustable glass louvers. The front room window covered a whole wall. With the sky blue walls and the curtains of blue, sprinkled with little nosegays of a deeper hue I thought the whole affair quite gorgeous! They were not so gorgeous when I had to wash the windows – a good 100 separate panes.

We had a little building at the back, half of it was set-up with sinks for a wash house and the other to store wood. The other homes had larger ones and were used for hired girls in times past. Many a story could be told of the voluptuous island girls who lived in them and hot blooded Polagi men – I imagine the wives, alone in their beds, could tell a story or two as well!

We had a huge yard at the back with two Flame trees and a banana tree. A lovely patio completed the front where we would sit in the warm evenings. The patio was fringed with Frangipani plants, Hibiscus, Periwinkle here and there, and a huge variegated bush which I'd cut back every five months but it grew so quickly it spread over the patio.

I had three flower boxes built by a local carpenter, Bill brought some soil from the farm and I planted seeds from home as well as some purchased locally. The morning glorys from home were a huge success. I'd plant the seeds and they were up in three days, in bloom in two weeks and finished in a month. Then I'd pick off the seeds and start again. The masses of blue flowers even matched my curtains. My I felt clever!

Many Polagis tried to grow little gardens and some succeeded to a point. But there is very little soil on Niue, a depth of six or seven inches is considered wonderful so you had to haul soil. Exotic insects didn't help either. You had to absolutely *love* gardening or it just wasn't worth the work. I didn't.

But what I did love was the huge chilli pepper bush which was always loaded with those hot delights, in various stages. When Bill saw my pepper bush he just about had a major fit. You see, he hates spices of any kind. If I put as much as a bay leaf in my stew his hair curls. In fact if I even salt and pepper an egg I have to do it when he's not watching. I love lots of spices in food and add them when he's outside, and he never notices but if he sees me with a spice jar he shorts out! So you can imagine his reaction when I glowingly showed him my pepper bush.

"You wouldn't Bets."

"Try me!"

I didn't use many chillis but Rosie, my Sri Lankan friend, used chillis all the time and picked them sometimes while still green, but they were extremely *hot!* both green and red. If I got a hankering for hot food I would run up when she was cooking and taste everything – her curries were marvelous.

When we first moved in I had planned on doing all my own housework but in due time and after many sore bones from scrubbing cement floors I went with the flow and had a house-girl come in for a half day once a week.

Sa was my first one. She was terribly shy, so shy it bothered me as well as her. If company dropped in while she was there, she disappeared. One day Jane McNamara popped in. Jane was the Resident Representative's wife and a real lady. Sa disappeared and was banging about the bedroom calling to me to bring her soap, water and whatever she needed. I made tea and I called Sa to join us – she did quite reluctantly. Jane chatted to her, hoping to put her at ease but the tea rattled in her cup, and her one leg took on a life of its own and knocked over the scrubbing pail. I felt sorry for her but she wasn't as nervous as I thought. When Jane left, Sa walked to the window to see her drive off, and said with much bravado "Well, well, that woman's some nervous ain't she!"

After Sa left Uga came. Uga the Ebullient, what a marvellous character! I had a western style broom but Uga wasn't about to use it – she brought her own Niuean broom until I bought one. These are made from the midrib or spine of the coconut leaf, a group are tied together and called a "Kaniu."

Uga never missed a thing. She knew all the juiciest gossip and embellished each story with suitable gestures, many just missing vulgarity by a scratch.

She had great faith in the old time native remedies for illnesses as most elderly Niueans did. There was much good in these herbal cures. Even the doctors would go to an old village lady for medicine if they were ill.

Uga would sweep through, dust, and scrub and if time permitted iron. I'd make lunch and then I'd drive her home. Part of her family lived in New Zealand and wanted her to move there but she'd thought better of it: "They just want a free babysitter! I'm staying on my island!"

After Uga left I hired a gentle young girl, Elaine. She was good and thorough, rather like a soft breeze after Uga's whirlwind.

The main town, like our settlement, was set in a semi-circle with the green in the centre. The radio station was at the bottom of a hill with the ocean right on its doorstep. The main Niuean church was perched at the top which was full to brimming each and every Sunday. The Parliament Buildings were also on the main stretch, and sat on the edge of a cliff overlooking the Pacific.

There were two main stores downtown. Burns Philp sold groceries, dry goods and hardware. Everyday there would be motorbikes leaning on its weathered exterior while the natives in bright prints and thongs visited within. There were piles of bush knives in the corner, fishing gear suitable for wild water, Polynesian prints galore as well as all other doo dads common to island stores.

The other main store downtown was owned by the Rex family and was much the same and sold the same goods as BPs. The Rex family were powerful, holding many positions on the Island. Robert Rex, the patriarch of the family was first elected Premier in 1975 and still held that post while we were there. He was knighted by Queen Elizabeth in 1983 so he is Sir Robert Rex. One son owned the Crab Inn and a daughter-in-law was the superintendent of the radio station when we arrived. Another daughter-in-law worked in Central Office.

Farther up past the hotel is another large store, K mart. It is privately owned by the Kar family, Russel Kar married a Niuean and they, along with three daughters ran the store.

One thing about the shops in Niue, they are clean. The shelves are kept dusted and the windows shining. The cement floors were polished to such a degree your life was in your hands walking on them, especially if you had regular shoes on.

Just across from our settlement was a club, "The Top Club," with a golf green as well as a tennis court. Whites can join this club as well as Niueans. But what amused me was, behind this exclusive club was the prison! It's not a prison with watch towers, fences and guards as we know prisons. In fact it's very "laid back." If you were playing tennis the prisoners would be there watching, hooting, hollering and cheering. Most of the inmates would be given leave to go home over the weekend with the stipulation they stay away from liquor and go to church on Sunday!

The slaughterhouse was in the same area and a clothing factory where you could take material and have it made up by one of three or four seamstresses. The lady in charge of the factory also ran a screen printing business. At the back of the building a New Zealander had a woodworking shop where he built dining room sets out of the very lovely Niuean wood.

Nearby was the factory which processed limes and passion fruit for juice and coconuts for coconut cream. This factory was run by Gary Cooper, a very likeable, gregarious character, married to the Premier's daughter, Tina.

The island itself was small, only about sixty-four kilometres around the outside. If your vehicle ran right you could completely encircle it in two hours. I received many letters wondering how we could stand staying on such a little place for two years – wasn't it confining? Speaking for myself, I never felt confined in any way. Any time I wished I could go out to the small native villages which surrounded the island. The route was always interesting. You would pass through plantations or bush gardens, rain forest, and all sorts of lookout spots from where you had magnificent views of the vast Pacific. Somehow I never tired of this trip. Many times of course I just went to one village or out to the farm but believe me I was never, ever bored.

Fualahi

Niue was unique in so many ways and our way of life there equally unique. It seemed to me we lived in two different worlds all on this tiny island!

There was our own little settlement comprised for the most part of all whites from New Zealand. Each family there on a posting for two years. So there were always families leaving and new ones arriving, but as we had found when in Tanzania, you make friends very quickly and very deeply if you are at all compatable.

But during the day I found myself out of the settlement mixing with the Niuean population, either shopping, visiting, teaching crafts and learning, learning, learning; returning by late afternoon to be with Bill and mixing with the families in our settlement. Of course this set pattern overlapped at times but this was the basic picture.

What Bill and I noticed from the start was the New Zealanders (the main influence in our settlement) spoke with such an accent and so very softly we didn't have a clue what they were saying. You can only bluff so much. Bill has a problem hearing at the best of times, the result of spending too much time on noisy old tractors and machinery. He also had a terrible head cold and his ears were still humming from the flight for well over a week, so he had a terrible time. Most times he'd look to me to decipher but I was in the same boat. My hearing's fine, at least I thought so until then, but I couldn't understand a thing. They'd be talking about the government or the Falkland's War and Bill would shout, "Hey, it's great weather!" and I was no better. The first few weeks we noticed many weird looks and a drawing back of warm bodies! But still in our favour, the new Zealanders have a habit of dropping the last three words of their sentences — so you were left with four words which head most anywhere! Like "When are you going to the library" could be, "When are you going shopping, to bed, to the reef?"

Also, they answer your questions with "Hmms" — and each cadence means something different, long ones, short ones, high ones, low ones. We didn't stand a chance. The New Zealanders were of course having great difficulty with us and our inflections.

Another area which really threw me was their expressions. Even when I could hear them and figure out their "Hmms" I still had problems. Their thongs are "jandals," a wrench is a "spanner," the trunk of a car is a "boot," pancakes are "pikelets," burs on your socks are called "biddy bits," and chickens are "chooks." I too have some weird and wonderful expressions which are rarely heard in Canada, never mind around the world. So you can well imagine the uproar until we all settled in.

But the hardest for me was the identification of meals. Back home on the farm we have breakfast, dinner and supper with coffee breaks in between. But while there, breakfast I could slip by — I got up at five a.m. and could call it anything I wanted. Everyone else was still in bed and our dinner was lunch, that I could handle but after that was a magnificent headache.

One of my new friends popped over at five p.m. "Come for tea," she said. I had been scrubbing all day and was in my grungy shorts but I *needed* that cup of tea. So I said "I'll be right over." I noticed she gave me a funny look but I thought she was reacting to my dirty shirt and it did run through my mind it was a strange time for tea, but I shouted to Bill I was going for a cup of tea. I wiped my feet, ran a comb through my hair and wandered over. Glory be! When I got there the front parlor was loaded with people dressed to kill and my little hostess looked like an island queen! The table was decked in white linen, silver candlesticks and flowers. I muttered something about "a pretty fancy cup of tea" and retreated in shame, tripping over Topsey, the dog. I learn quickly, especially when I pull such a gigantic boner. I showered and dressed and swept across the green to attend a *Tea!* Other than a few funny looks everyone was kind enough to ignore my blunder.

Still I had to learn, if it was a fancier affair, which I couldn't see how it could be, it's then called Dinner, and if lunch is served after an evening of visiting it is called Supper. So you can understand my bewilderment! But for the next few days I drilled myself all day. "Tea is Supper, Dinner, high class tea and after ten snack is Supper." I can memorize much easier if I talk out loud so as I was chopping wood, peeling vegetables, or sitting on the toilet I'd be reciting "Tea, Lunch, Dinner." I had to quit, however, when the next door neighbour thought I had a man hidden somewhere in the house!

Many of the families in our settlement became very dear friends and wonderful were the times we had together. Right across the green for our house lived the Airport Superintendent and his wife, Barry and Tui Waters.

Barry was a stocky, solid New Zealander, a cross between Sir Winston Churchill and a Welsh tavern keeper. He had worked as a telegraphist for years in New Zealand and transferred to the Air Nautical Department, a job which took him to several tropical islands. He met his wife, an island girl, when posted in Rarotonga.

Barry's hobby was playing with his ham radio. If the night was clear, you could hear him tapping out the various codes. He also had a passion for the video tapes which could be rented downtown. A lot of these were TV programs from New Zealand. Bill and I could tell when Barry was watching his all time favourite "Benny Hill" when we heard great guffas of laughter emitting from their home.

However, we could always tell when Barry had a rough day. He had started constructing packing cases to use when his term was up but each bad day he'd attack them with gusto, swearing away as he banged in the nails.

Barry was liked by the Niuean people and had a good friendly relationship with many of them. But the place where Barry really shone in my eyes was in his relationship with Tui. He was so good to her, not that she didn't deserve it, she did, but he was extra special.

Tui was diagnosed as having Parkinson's disease, and was at one time even confined to a wheelchair. Tui though has courage, grit and never gives up. Tui's determination combined with a change of doctors and treatment, and Barry always there to coach and cajole, she overcame her ailment to such a degree she was not only walking and working but also playing tennis so well she could, and did, beat anyone in the tournaments held at the Top Club.

Tui was petite, beautiful, and a lady through and through. It didn't seem to matter what she wore, tennis outfit, evening gown or a pareau, her beauty, both internal and external shone through.

It just seemed natural that Tui and I would team up; we were "soul mates." The extent of this is exampled through a dream I had one night. Only one and so clear I can see it yet. I dreamt I was outside near the lane and a little white owl came and sat on a post near my head. It just sat there looking at me with wise eyes. When I woke in the morning I couldn't get it out of my mind. It was more than a dream. I didn't see Tui until that evening which in itself was strange. Leigh and Bob were having a B.B.Q. and when I sat down I started telling Leigh my weird dream. I saw this owl so clearly! Tui looked at me and said, "Betsy, that was my mother saying goodbye. She passed away last night and came to you!"

I'll never forget it.

Tui was industrious, always working at some project or another. She made beautiful quilts, Rarotongan style, rather like our log cabin pattern ones. These were made out of cotton of brilliant colours, with many seams. She made Bill and I a pair which are on our bed now.

Tui also loved to entertain. She hauled rocks and gravel about, built a patio out back and set up a B.B.Q. area –

coloured lights and all. At a drop of a hat she would plan a B.B.Q. I used to tell her "If the moon was full she'd hold a party." "And when it's not full too, Betsy!" she'd laugh.

Our good friends Barry and Tui Waters

A third family became part of our circle, the Kammanankada's; Rosie and Godfrey and their two sons, James and Archer. They were also on Niue as volunteers from their home country of Sri Lanka.

Godfrey was a gentleman of the old order, extremely clever and just plain nice. The two boys, five and three-years-old when we arrived, were beautiful children and Rosie kept them spotless and dressed to perfection – shoes shining, pants pressed and sparkling white shirts. They had a young boy's love of everything western; cowboys being one of their favourite heros. I remember making them two cowboy neckerchiefs out of old remnants, really weird colours but I thought for the world of make-believe they'd be fine. To my horror I saw the boys the following Sunday going off to church in their grey flannels and white shirts with the kerchiefs tied proudly around their necks!

Rosie was quite shy, tiny and pretty with an infectious giggle that was always just below the surface ready to pop out.

She was a very traditional Sri Lankan wife living in the background but after she became involved with Tui and I, who are anything but traditional, she started breaking free of some of her ideas. She was also a hairdresser and had quite a business going in her home. Many Niueans and whites couldn't have managed without her talented hands.

Another couple who played a big role in our lives lived next door to us. They were Annette and Paul Gatland and their two children, Jon and Nikki. Paul, a tall handsome reserved fellow worked with civil service in New Zealand and worked at Central Office on Niue.

Bill and I have four daughters and one daughter-in-law and subconsiously, I was collecting replacements to have while there and Annette was one very like my own. Annette was pregnant when we arrived and Jon was two and a half years old. Jon was very shy and it took him a long time to dig up enough courage to come over and knock on our door. At first he'd just sit on the floor playing with some old chunks of foam I had, never a smile but in due time he was popping in with a great grin. He still hadn't met Bill when one Saturday Bill was sitting reading by the window when Jon came over and spotted him and went home mad as he could be. "What's wrong Jon?" Annette asked. "Betty has an old man in there!" he snorted.

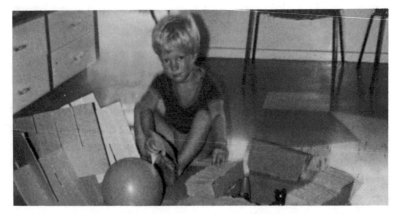

Little Jon was very special.

Of course Bill and Jon became great friends and shared a milkshake each day when Bill came home from work. Nikki was born on Niue and was also coming over by the time the Gatland's returned to New Zealand.

Mr. Z and his wife lived in our settlement when we first arrived, and as I mentioned before was Bill's boss. They left quite soon after we arrived and maybe it was a good thing. Mr. Z was one of those Englishmen who feel that England is the world centre and anyone else is just not as good. We being Canadians, were colonists therefore not up to English standards. I being half Irish didn't take kindly to this pompous attitude and he and I had an understanding – we hated each other. Of course, I had inadvertantly called him "a dirty old goat" one evening and this didn't relieve tensions. He also hurt my friends Rosie and Godfrey, who lived next door to him. One day he went over to Rosie, when Godfrey was at work, and told her he was sure she'd be much happier moving out of the settlement, possibly to one of the native villages seeing as how she was of a different race. She might be hurt by the racial slurs etcetera by the rest of the whites in the area. Rosie never even answered him, she was so surprised. But there wasn't one other family there who even thought such nonsense. Whether he really felt he had their best interests at heart or not I don't know. I know I felt it was out and out of racial prejudice.

Mr. Z was not liked by the Niueans, and that was an explosive situation. If you got on the wrong side of the Niuean population you had problems. When Mr. and Mrs. Z went on a three week holiday to islands west, their baggage was sent east. It didn't get together with Mr. Z until he was back on Niue after his three week holiday. Bill asked the baggage handler how this could happen? The handler gazed up at the heavens and intoned in a solemn voice and twinkle in his eye, "An act of God! Bill, an act of God!"

But in the end the unhappy union between Mr. Z and Niue ended abruptly when a strike was called. I had noticed pickups full of men heading to Z's house at funny hours for several days. The men at the farm didn't know what they were striking for, nor did some even know what a strike was. But it meant time off from work and a little excitement which was, admittedly, lacking at times on the island. Bill, however, went out to the farm each day and fed and tended the stock. But it was over quickly. Mr. Z was charged with inciting a strike and Premier Rex ordered him off the island within twenty-four-hours. And Malcolm, the Resident Representative escorted Mr. Z rather unceremoniously up the steps and into the plane. I thought after, that it was a good thing there was a plane that day or Mr. Z would have been paddling a canoe in the Pacific heading for Samoa.

Soon after, Bruce Reid, a New Zealand school teacher moved into the vacated house. His nature was the exact opposite of Mr. Z's. We just loved him. His wife, Eileen, was still working in New Zealand and couldn't join him for a year. Bruce was such a gentle and wonderful person I just knew Eileen would have to be the same.

I made a bet with Bill the day her plane was to arrive. "She'll be tiny, with dark hair, have a cotton wrap-around skirt on and have a guitar hung on her back." The only thing I missed was her guitar – she was carrying it in a case! I should have bet for money! She also was the offspring of an Irish father and had the "Fay" spirit of her Irish ancestry. Anyway, Eileen became my second daughter, I had two to go.

Our gentle friends Bruce and Eileen Reid.

One interesting couple was Ruth and Duncan Miller. I'm not sure exactly what Duncan did other than work through Central Office, but what I do know was he was a rather wonderful character and fit my dream of what a white civil servant should be like on a strange Polynesian Island. Shades of Kipling and Michener again!

He was a slight man, always a gentleman and always hustling about. They were extremely hospitable and many were the wonderful meals we had at the Millers. They had twin boys about two years old when we arrived and they really kept Ruth hopping. She was a kindergarten teacher and felt her whole time should be devoted to teaching her little boys – even if housework was left. Once or twice a week when the house was a total disaster she had a native lady come in to give it a thorough going though. I personally feel if you have anything else worthwhile to do leave the house – it won't walk away. In fact I have a little verse up on my kitchen wall in Alberta right beside the back door which states; "Those that let the small things bind them leave the great undone behind them" which I can gaze upon when I leave many a mess in my home. So you will understand when I say I was in full agreement with Ruth. Anyway, if they were having guests for dinner Duncan would do the cooking. And what Culinary delights he served up – he was a marvelous cook. But the joy of eating the food was not the only delight when we were invited to the Miller's. What I really enjoyed was watching the preparation.

Duncan usually had kicked off his sandals (or should I say "jandals") and would be bustling about the little kitchen; khaki shorts, shirt tail half out, spoon in one hand and a full glass of wine in the other which he sipped at while he furiously stirred the aromatic dishes. He was something to behold!

Another couple who were there when we arrived were Bob and Leigh Sutton. Bob worked with telecommunications and like Barry was a ham radio nut – he just loved it, much to perfectionist Leigh's chagrin. He would lay out all his wonderful bits and pieces all over the floor.

Leigh's Dad was a Maori and her Mother an English lady, and she felt drawn to learn as much as possible about her father's heritage while on Niue. It was Leigh who helped make my curtains when I first arrived and it was Leigh who put on the farewell for us when we were leaving – I'll tell more of this latter.

Leigh was able to get off the island several times for the breaks she seemed to need. In fact a lot of the New Zealanders were able to go home for leave several times while we were there. Especially the young wives out of New Zealand for the first time. They would become down and homesick, then after being home for a couple of months would come back, bright and cheerful and glad to be back. It seemed after the breaks they could handle the little irritating things that bothered them about the island.

The rest of our settlement were all different and all nice and we all got along extremely well for being so different and confined to such small areas. Of course people were coming and going all the while and some who came were dreadful, others wonderful. It seems anyone who goes abroad on a posting has to be different – you have to be a character and we all were. There seemed to evolve two groups within the settlement – swingers and squares. The swingers really swung – even to spouse swapping. They were all having a marvelous time, and it helped break a dull evening for the squares too.

While we stayed with our own partners we had great fun sitting on our respective patios in the evening to see who went into who's house with their PJs slung over their arm! Just like going to the movies. We'd even serve cold drinks in the intermission. For a double feature we had to rise early to see who came out of who's house. I have the feeling that when posted to a small island where no one knows you or your place in society at home, you tend to go to extremes and do things you wouldn't even consider in your own society.

I quickly realized the peculiar forces surrounding us. We were quite cut off from the outside world; people, all characters in their own right with widely separated ideas, viewpoints and moral standards were thrown into close, not to mention intimate, contact. Under ordinary circumstances in our own world we would have travelled in different circles probably never meeting. Here, however, we mingled in a boarding house atmosphere so of course there were eruptions!

There was another small area at the bottom of our hill where other Polagis lived. It was in this area I found the other two girls who were my daughters in spirit.

One couple Steven and Yvonne, with their two little girls, Michelle and Linda were very down to earth. Yvonne, a farm girl, was cheerful, energetic and loved Niue. Steven worked for Public Works. Of course their kids I also claimed as grandchildren. Michelle, the youngest, was a little character, cute as can be – to her we were "Uncle Betty and Bill." Linda was a beautiful quiet child and very clever. They both adapted into Niuean lifestyle and school with great ease. Of course Steven and Yvonne lived like Niueans, built an Umu in the back yard and had a bush garden as well as chickens and a lot of their close friends were Niuean.

My last daughter I found in an apartment across from Yvonne – Sue O'Shea and her husband Gary. Sue was absolutely beautiful, tall and slim. Gary was a teacher and was as handsome as Sue was beautiful. I really loved them and we spent lovely hours together.

Sue and Gary lived in the same apartment block as Jansie Sharplin. Jansie had come to teach on Niue in the latter part of our term. She was from a commune in Port Charles, New Zealand and all the people in the commune took turns going out to work to help keep the commune going. Well, Sue and Gary had their bed up against her living room wall. She kept late hours and just before going to bed she played a "way out" beat on her Indian drums. Poor Sue, one night she was desperately trying to sleep but the tom' bom' bom' started up.

She lay there plugging her ears but it didn't work. Finally, in desperation, she got up and walked to the door and was about to yell out her suffering but being such a kind creature, couldn't and turned about and walked back. It went on and on,

Sue told me the next time she was going to take a couple of pots and pans and bang them under Jansie's bedroom window.

Jansie, like every commune member – dressed casually in rather weird outfits that somehow suited her. She also had the typical thinking of commune people. She had embraced Buddism as her religion and was ecstatic about it. One time we were all at the hotel for some special occasion. Rosie, Tui and I were sitting together and Jansie spotted Rosie, who looks very East Indian, whipped up to her and said, "Hi, I'm Jansie! I'm Buddist!" thinking for sure Rosie was too. Rosie sat back in amazement and said shakily, "Oh, I'm Rosie – I'm, I'm Catholic!"

When we arrived there were (including us) eight UN people on the island. Doris Wong who travelled with us, was working in Treasury; Trini, a Philipino married to the secretary to the New Zealand representative, was a lab technician; Leo another Philipino; a tall Dutch girl who worked in Field Corps and who was having a rip snorting affair with Mr. Z.; and Tony, a Belgian, was also a Field Corps Specialist.

Tony was a quiet person, very gentle. He went to Niger after he left Niue. The posting came suddenly and he was in a real dilemma as he had but forty-eight-hours to tidy up and get his affairs in order. He was so desperate he ran up and asked me if I'd help him pack. Little did he know how dreadful I am at packing! I'm truly the world's worst. Then to top it off there was a Niuean fellow also in attendance. I think he was to help me but he mostly sat on a packing case chatting while I rolled dishes in paper. Tony had such nice dishes too. I finally finished but was positive when he opened his trunk in Niger he'd find 10,000 pieces. But he and his family visited us this year and only one wine glass was broken – I couldn't believe it. I don't, however, plan on going to McCoshams for a job.

And then there was Jim Butler. Jim, a draftsman by trade, was one of my very favourite people on the island. He is an Irishman from Dublin and had all the virtues and vagaries and all the wonderful agents of his Irish ancestry. It is hard to describe Jim and do him justice. He is brilliant and can discuss with great intelligence any subject you can dream up. He is also an outdoorsman, into mountain climbing and hiking, and an unmerciful mimic. Being Irish he could also get very irate about anything that bugged him, the UN red tape, Niuean politics. He did not abide fools easily, as the saying goes.

It didn't matter what the problem was Jim could fix it. Bill always carried a pocket watch, and often dropped it on the cement. As a result the second hand was bent causing all sorts of problems. Jim took the second hand right out and tied a good solid string in the knob so Bill could hang it on his belt.

He was a good photographer too, and had probably the best and most extensive collection of slides on Niue. Whatever Jim did he did wholeheartedly. His shell collection was documented and in trays, his butterfly collection the same. He was out hiking over the island nearly every day and by the time he left he had explored every nook and cranny. When I was driving, I'd meet him marching along, red plastic sandals, shorts, carrying an umbrella, his piercing blue eyes and his beard and hair flowing in the wind. He reminded me of a prophet from the Old Testament. I imagined Moses looking like that as he parted the Red Sea. And boy could he walk!

Godfrey, being a surveyor, spent a good deal of time marching around in the forest and felt he was fit. So when Jim invited him to go on a hike to the other end of the island he said "Sure." The next morning when we saw Rosie she was giggling away, Godfrey could barely get out of bed he was so sore. She had to help him to the bathroom where he sat groaning away.

I loved an evening or afternoon when Jim came. He'd rarely have time to stop for a meal but some how I'd badger him into it and I'm glad. Conversation was always bright when he was there. He was so Irish it brought out my emerald streak and we had many an Irish chuckle at the expense of others.

As time went on I got to know the New Zealand Resident Representative and his wife, Malcolm and Jane McNamara. They also were wonderful characters. Malcolm was a geologist and had worked in the diplomatic corp in New Zealand. His wife had had a like position before they married so both were intelligent people. They were fun too. Usually I remember not so much the important things but a myriad of funny little ones and it is so with this couple.

Most all New Zealanders are gentlemen but Malcolm personified this trait. He was charming and gallant to the *nth* degree. It didn't matter what happened he didn't lose his cool or get in a flap (or as a New Zealander would say, "Get his knickers in a knot.") I remember a story Annette told me. Annette and Paul had Jane and Malcolm over for bridge with Annette paired up with Malcolm. Annette said she's really not a poor bridge player but this time she was tired or something and proceeded to pull boner after boner, each time Malcolm said nothing. Finally she finished off with a really *stupid* move. Any other partner would have cussed, but not Malcolm. He raised one elegant eyebrow and stated in his New Zealand accent; "My, that is an unusual move."

Jane and Malcolm McNamara.

Another time he was asked to say grace at a gathering at the hotel. There were lots of Niueans there as well as whites. Not to be thrown, Malcolm said it in Latin. One thing Bill noticed about Malcolm was if he needed his assistance, whatever needed doing, he did it quickly and well. He was a character and I told Jane this one day and she replied: "That's why I married him Betty."

Jane was as perfect for her position as Resident Representative's wife as Malcolm was as Resident Representative. She had the dignity and stamina required for such a posting plus a good share of humour which was an absolute necessity. I believe those, and there were very few who didn't care for Jane, were actually afraid of her and what her position represented. She was a tall blond lady, forever in command of herself. But many a wonderful visit we had. She'd drive up in her big car and pop in for a quick cup of tea, but somehow we'd always drain the pot and more often than not make another. The first time or two I worried if the house was a mess, but it didn't matter to Jane or me either.

One memorable time, Jane stopped in when Laurel, a Mormon missionary friend stationed on Niue, was there and I was in the middle of giving her a home perm. We sat about visiting while we waited for the perm to process, the conversation switched to birth control (I felt, after thinking it over, Jane plotted the whole thing) Anyway, Jane sat straight and tall and stated, "I feel some people think condoms are sausage skins." I just about came unwound, Laurel was caught unawares and blushed furiously, while Jane looked smug! Of course Jane and I had not discussed condoms but both felt that if the teenage Niuean girls could avoid having children before marriage they'd have a better chance at finishing their education and possibly fulfilling other goals they might set for themselves in various fields of endeavor. I know many Niueans I talked to felt the same way.

While stationed on Niue Jane spent a good deal of time helping with a UN project which was to encourage the ladies of Niue to continue to weave traditional patterns by traditional methods. It was hoped to establish a record of the various types of weaving. Young Vivian, Jane's co-worker, and Jane hoped to persuade the women to weave some of the very old patterns and teach the younger women, so the pattern and know how wouldn't fade from memory. Jane felt it tragic that many of the Niuean's finest and oldest artifacts are now in museums in Britain and New Zealand, Australia and Germany, although they are probably safer in these museums. Some were taken by people who worked on Niue. Their project was aimed at locating these artifacts. Jane did manage to locate some and had indeed received catalogue cards and photographs from museums around the world. The Otago museum in New Zealand returned a magnificent Tapa clock which now hangs in the Fale fono (Parliament building).

The Wanderings Beyond

Once we were settled into our home, had met our neighbours and I had managed to drive down the main drag and back without serious mishap the time was right to venture forth and explore the island and its peoples. I certainly wasn't going to stay within the confines of our settlement sheltered though I might have been.

My car and I had developed a dubious respect for each other − neither expecting too much. It was probably the most dilapitated vehicle on the island and possibly the smallest. The seat covers were in threads with great gaping holes and stuffing hanging out, the wipers didn't work nor did the signal lights also there was the fact of the gap about an inch wide between the body and the floor all along one side and half way around the other. I had great visions of losing the floor completely and possibly Rosie and Tui along with it.

The back seat wouldn't stay hooked and when I braked it sprung forward just about throwing the passengers in the back onto my knees. When I drove up a hill the wheels were so poorly aligned they would go sideways rather like a crab. I also noticed the serial number had been chiselled off. The story behind that I never heard because the car had passed through many owners.

There were a few times my car gave me trouble − flat tires or boiling over but once I had gone over a really rough section of road to visit a plant nursery and on the way back I heard weird rumblings underneath and the odd thump. I just kept going − there wasn't much else I could do. I turned into our settlement and just 100 yards from home it gave a final groan and I heard a great clunk. Bill had just arrived home and heard the racket and ran out of the house just in time to see not only the muffler but four or five feet of pipe and all land on the road. He just laughed.

But even though the state of my car was the object of much amusement, many who laughed were forced to borrow it when their finer vehicles refused to run! One obstacle I had to overcome, not only for my safety but also the safety of the population at large, was learning to drive on the opposite side of the road. I really worried about this, but Bill reminded me, all I had to do was remember to keep the steering wheel always in the centre of the road. This worked like a charm when I kept my wits about me but many times I'd be off on a cloud and would suddenly realize I was also on the wrong side. I'm sure a warning had gone out over the land; "Look out for the white Mama in the little green car!" The odd soul would be forced to skip quickly aside or run up the Post Office steps but other than that all went well. I had a wonderful thing in my favour though – we had bought the car from the Police Chief so no matter what I did wrong in the way of poor driving practices I never got stopped.

We did have to purchase Niuean drivers licenses, but no test was taken. Possibly they were all afraid to drive with me, but I like to think they trusted I wasn't a real hazard to life. When I received my license I had a thrill of thrills. Under occupation was marked "student." I showed it to Bill remarking,

"I must look younger than I thought!"

Bill completely discouraged such thoughts when he replied, "They think you're still learning to drive Bets!"

One of my first trips was out to the farm where Bill spent each and every day. He told me the shortest and best route, and gave me money for gas before he went off one morning. "Go slow Bets, and gun it on the Avatele Hill" he shouted as he hurried out in the early mist.

About 10:00 a.m. I set forth on my first adventure. Once I got past the filling station the scenery changed from the open view of the ocean to lovely quiet deep forest. It was beautiful. I drove slowly over the little winding road through the huge trees. There would be the odd peep of ocean blue, then all would be enclosed in green once more.

I had two good sized villages to go through before the farm and as I passed them all the ladies who were out on their morning chores would smile and wave. I wondered as I waved back if I'd get to know them and their ways and more importantly to me, if they would accept me as a friend.

Just before reaching the farm I came to what I thought was a deserted village – I wondered why it was vacated.

Soon I saw the farm and drove in. I'm not sure what I expected, an Alberta farm possibly, but it certainly was like no farm I'd ever seen anywhere. There were rows and rows of coconut trees, tall and towering with the cattle pasturing beneath them.

*The cattle pastured under the palms, keeping the grass
short for easier coconut harvesting.*

I drove up to the little office and Bill met me. I was introduced to all the workers, had a cup of coffee and went back
home. This was my first adventure – the beginning, but there
were many more. I wanted very much to mix with the Niueans
and learn from them and I plotted and planned how to best go
about this. I knew from my African experience to try to meet
them on their turf, I was the stranger, so I should try to meet
them not the other way around.

I was lucky in one way. Rosie, Tui and I always travelled
downtown always together. One white, one Islander and one
Sri Lankan – so we were the odd ones and the people realized
my best friends were not all whites. We soon identified as the
three always together and people discussed this. Bill would be
told out at the farm "Betty's best friends are not Polagis – that
is good!" Of course it was great for me too, for I couldn't have
found better company than Tui and Rosie.

We seemed to run downtown nearly every day and I soon
got to know the storekeepers, and the clerks and the people in

various offices. We hit every store each time we went downtown, to visit, look over the island fabrics etc. I particularly liked to go into Rex's General Store. Patricia, the Premier's wife was in charge. She ran it well too, opening it herself early each morning. Her office was boxed in a corner built up a few feet with stairs leading up to it. She would sit up there, working on her books and keeping everything running smoothly.

Patricia Rex was a solid lady with sharp eyes peeking out of her rimmed glasses missing absolutely nothing. She reminded me of a tiny owl sitting on her perch surveying her domain. If her books were up-to-date she'd be busy crocheting or doing embroidery and if she wanted to chat she'd shout out and wave her hand as you came in the door. I rather liked to stand back and just watch her she was so compelling. After a few visits I felt quite at ease with her and could just skip up the steps to talk. I always found these visits enjoyable as she was a good conversationalist endowed with a great sense of humour and a lot of common sense. Patricia Rex worked long and hard for the women of the island and was respected by them.

A Hurricane? Wonderful!!

The weather in Niue was just right most of the time. That is, just right for me. From April to November we had warm sunny days with a temperature about twenty to twenty-three degrees Celsius. During those months a person could comfortably wear skirts and shirts without feeling the heat.

In fact the evenings could be chilly and you would need a light sweater and only in the evenings I could wear slacks. Bill had to be off to work at 6:30 in the cooler season and I remember getting up to find a ground fog and heavy mist on everything. The cement floors would be so cold I had to put on socks to warm my feet. Of course by 9:00 or so it would be warm and lovely once more.

The hot season however is a different thing – I'd have to get Bill off to work at 5:30, and its a good thing, because if I had any real household chores like baking or ironing, it would get so hot I'd have to complete it before 9:00 or 9:30. The temperature itself wasn't desperately high, 36 degrees was the hottest I remember, but the humidity was intense. The monthly average, taken at 7:00 a.m., was 90.48. I well remember sitting with Tui over a cold drink at 9:00 a.m. in just shorts or brief sundress and the water pouring off us.

The extreme humidity not only played havoc with humans it also raised all sorts and colours of mold on any handy objects. The walls and curtains were well decorated with mold, as were shoes, suitcases and any clothing not in daily use. The larger homes had one huge closet with a heat lamp which kept mildew and mold at bay but we didn't have such a thing so I spent a great deal of time airing everything out. Even my leatherbound bible was covered in mold. Of course Bill figured, and probably rightly so, this was caused by lack of use.

One thing in favour of humidity – you could keep cigarettes for months on an open shelf and they'd stay moist. I also noticed my skin, usually extra dry, was soft as was my hair, it sounds like an "Oil of Olay" commercial but it was true. Even though we suffered from the humidity we were told it could be much worse. The year we arrived Niue was in the throes of the worst drought in recorded history. This was caused by El Nino.

El Nino is a phenomenon which happens in the Pacific every ten years. The cloud cover which normally drifts over the region from countries north and west of Australia, like New Guinea is lacking. As a result, the ocean water is heated to a much greater depth thus the ocean currents shift, causing great droughts throughout the whole Pacific, and South America even at times felt as far north as the Prairies of Canada. This was the cause of the terrible drought which not only hit Niue but also Australia, causing the terrible fires of 1982-83. It is said that El Nino was partly the cause of the drought in the 1930s in Canada.

Many days I had to take cold showers two or three times a day just to cool off. If I went downtown I found I was completely wiped-out by the time I got home. We went through jugs and jugs of passion fruit juice or squash. Most people drank lime juice but limes are terribly acidic and my ulcers would react to as much as a half a glass.

When it rained it cooled the air and we all looked forward to a good rain shower. I had anticipated the Rainy Season as days and days of steady torrential tropical downpour, but it wasn't to be. I only saw water puddles actually once or twice, and overnight rains were few and far between.

One little thing I loved was the fact that when the rains would come, never was there a bit of mud. I am so accustomed to Alberta rains which result in mud holes, mud on my porch, mud on my shoes and everywhere else, but there the rain ran right into the ground and through the porous rock underneath. It was glorious!

We were situated in the hurricane belt, a bit of a worry for the wiser of the Polagis but I had a secret wish to witness a hurricane. Not a "heller" but just enough to get the feel of it. I'd listen everyday to reports on short wave from New Zealand and Samoa and hope. I never breathed a word of this secret desire to a soul, and for good reason, I would probably be committed. Then one day it happened – about 2:00 p.m. a warning of a possible hurricane heading towards the island. Barry Waters got the word in the tower at the airport and was responsible for keeping both the Radio Station and our settlement informed. He got in his Landrover, turned on the siren and proceeded to inform all and sundry. To Barry it was serious work and he proceeded to fulfill his duty with great reverence and aplomb.

He stopped at my door and with solemity asked when Bill was expected, told me not to panic, but be ready. *Panic?* I was delighted. But I had to hold back my great mirth. I didn't want him to think me so horrid that I actually loved death and destruction! So I eyed him very bravely as he proceeded to tell me what to do to save me and mine:

> The power will probably go off so fill every vessel with water, check canned food supplies it may be days before supplies get to us. Check your torch and make sure you have batteries. Go through your First Aid Kit – You do have a First Aid Kit? (Actually my First Aid Kit was 4 bandaids, 2 *Dispirin*, (New Zealand Aspirin,) that the ants got to and some Dettol. But I didn't let on.) Above all Betsy do *not* go outside. The wind will sweep through and all will be still. Don't be fooled. We are then in the eye of the storm and it will swing back and blow just as devilish from the other direction. Get Bill to put up your storm shutters immediately! But do *not* panic! All will be well.

With that he marched off like Sir Winston Churchill to broadcast to the British.

The storm shutters were 3/4 inch plywood with a 2' by 4' frame and cut to fit each window. These were nailed on with huge spikes.

I met Bill with the great news, and he and Bob proceeded to nail them on. The little house took on a strange look. I could hear the hammering throughout our settlement and we met in little subdued groups discussing the event to be.

There was a real stillness in the air, not a breeze, as the whole island waited in readiness. Gosh it was exciting!

We waited and waited – nothing. I made supper or should I say dinner? and we ate it on the patio discussing which of the trees might be pulled up by the roots and tossed on the house top. By 8:00 p.m. Bill got tired of waiting and went off to bed. I stayed up until 9:00 p.m. and decided I'd better get a bit of sleep before the hurricane actually hit. But before I realized, I dropped off only to be woken by the alarm clock at 5:30 in the morning. The fool hurricane had gone by sixty miles out to sea. My, what a disappointment!

It was a cloudy, stormy day, just about as stormy as my thoughts. I ran into Paul and told him I heard the winds had been 120 kilometres per hour. Paul and Annette had lived on the east coast of New Zealand, and his reply was a " 'hmph,' that's just a breeze in Wellington!" I drove down to Alofi to mail some letters and as I came over Tapeu Hill I noticed the ocean. I had always seen it when it was tranquil and serene, rippling with little waves. This day it was raging! Great grey waves were beating against the cliffs, spilling over. I was mesmerized!

I hurried downtown and pulled in by the big church where there was a commanding view or the ocean. I believe it was in that moment I gained an immense respect for it. The power of the waves and the unearthly roar were unbelievable. A human being would be smashed against the cliffs like a straw if caught in one. In fact there had been accidents when storms brewed. While on Niue an uncle of one of the girls I would later work with was swept off an outcrop where he had been fishing and was drowned.

During one particular hurricane the waves were so high and the wind so strong that huge boulders and water were lifted over the cliff and carried a hundred yards or so through

Throw / dishclothes are
made from this. I
just wash dishclothes
with regular things
Potholders are heavier
cotton of same brand.

Pr **BEZALIP**®
400mg
ONCE-A-DAY / UNE FOIS PAR JOUR

the glass windows of the hotel lobby. The sunken dance floor became a wonderful pond for the surviving fish, where they were found swimming.

During the "cold" season I would be very comfortable in a blouse or cotton shirt while my Niuean friends would be freezing. The people coming to work on their motorbikes would be bundled up in ski jackets, put on backwards to keep the wind out, and many would have woolen tuques on. Babies would be bundled up with just their little dark eyes peeking out and the girls at the office, where I would work, would be shivering. I would try to explain, it was a "just right" day for me but they just put it down to another of my white idiosyncrasies, of which I had many!

Radio Sunshine? Other Adventures

After we were settled in I decided it was time to see if I could get a job. I wasn't sure what but I wanted to work with the Niueans. I really didn't have a lot to offer and I had been warned by the white population that no Polagi would be hired, never had been and I was silly to try. But that worked like a "Double Dare" of childhood days and gave me the impetus needed.

There were two positions I might have a chance of filling: a columnist once a week, or possibly a program over *Radio Sunshine*, the local radio station which broadcast a few hours a day. I had written columns for more years than I can remember as well as freelancing. I also had limited radio experience. So I dug out my letters of recommendation I had collected from my editors and headed off with some trepidation to the Information Office where both the radio and the paper were produced.

The station was a sparse three-room building with a closet-like control room. It was situated so close to the ocean you'd think a big wave would sweep it asunder. The equipment was extremely basic but it had rustic charm and lots of warmth.

There were promises of a grand new building up on the top of the hill, with the latest equipment to be partly built with the help of the Australian government. I was glad I was there before the move for it was a unique experience. The whole staff was made up of Niueans – mostly women. Lofa Rex, the Premier's daughter-in law, was the editor and radio manager.

I told her I was new on the island, wanted to work with the people and if she gave me a job they would improve both my physical and mental well being. I didn't quite beg but it came close. Handing her my recommendations I sat back while she studied them.

"Well Betty, what would you be willing to try?" she asked.

I tried in vain to keep my voice casual as I held back a mighty, "Anything!"

"I would be willing to try a fifteen minute childrens' broadcast." I hadn't even thought of until that moment! and didn't have the slightest clue as to an approach but knowing third world countries and their red tape and pace of life I felt I'd have ample time to prepare such a program.

"Fine, I'll check with Central Office and let you know. Possibly stop in next week and I may have news for you."

Not a definite positive answer to be sure but I left with a grin on my face and a spring in my step. I ran into the Police Chief John at the BP store and told him what had transpired.

The police on Niue had their own methods of policing and had rules and regulations which fit their island and its lifestyle. This was only right, it's their home. But to a Western eye they were certainly unique to say the least. There were about ten recruits from various villages, and they knew everyone and all about them. They were very helpful unless they figured you thought you were superior. Then look out. I remember one polagi who was terribly patronizing and tended to laugh at the island and its people. There was seldom a time she wasn't making and telling the white population how she had out smarted some Niuean. I met a policeman one day who had just had a run in with her and her obnoxious manner. "Betty, she thinks her s__ don't stink!" and I agreed wholeheartedly. She had her comeuppence however. The time came when everytime she drove downtown she was stopped on some charge or another. Her lights were dusty, she was parked too close to the curb − or too far from it, she was a danger to bikers! She was probably too vain to figure out what was going on but it was glorious to watch.

John congratulated me (rather presumptuously I felt seeing as how I didn't have the job yet but it gave me a little more confidence) and offered me the use of one of his office typewriters. I promised to pick it up and thanked him profusely. I was home but a few minutes when up drove a police van. They had delivered not only the typewriter but also paper and carbon. It was acts of special kindness like this that gave me great cause to love Niue and its people.

I went down to the station the next week, nothing, the week after, still no word from Central Office. Finally, I figured I had nothing to lose and went to Central Office myself.

The main hub of the island's governmental work world was Central Office located right in the centre of Alofi. This group of offices contained the police station, the bank, the post office, liquor store and many other offices. Here was where the communications office was situated and I got to know it and some of the workers very well. Lofa Misa worked there and we became good friends. Her mother worked at the switchboard and she was a wonderful character. I learned very quickly, if I needed to know where any one person was in a hurry, day or night, all I had to do was contact Lofa's mother! One time I had been home cleaning all day when on the spur of the moment I thought I'd run some prickly heat powder to Laurel who was suffering from a heat rash. Just as I drove up Laurel beckoned me, "Betty, there's a phone call for you!" I ran in, wondering how the operator found me; "Honey, it's your son from Canada and he's got good news!" Sure enough it was Ian informing me of the birth of a new namesake granddaughter! But for the life of me I couldn't figure out how the operator knew where I was. Not a soul knew I was going to Laurels and the telephone office is farther on so she didn't see me pass – talk about coconut telegraph.

I found the man in charge and placed yet another plea. To make the long story short I did get the job and I had the fun of preparing and delivering a childrens' broadcast once a week over Niue radio.

It was a unique experience in a unique setting. My limited

radio experience was gained at the large CBC centre in Edmonton where I aired a short program once a week. I'd travel there once a month and tape my programs ahead of time. It was all spit and polish and very professional. *Radio Sunshine* was none of these. What it was, was fun. There were times when I'd go in to tape and the microphone would be missing or the turntable out of order, but I'd just go later and do a live program – no sweat.

While waiting for word on this job I decided on a theme song, followed by a greeting, a childrens' song, a story, another song and to close I figured a Magic Mirror which I'd look through and see the children listening. I decided I'd name all the little children in a different village each week, taking turns of course. (I later ran into trouble when the children would want to see my Magic Mirror. I would be hard pressed to explain that no one else could see it.) I had to collect all the names of the kids from each and every village on the whole island. But at that time I was so full of enthusiasm I didn't realize the work this would entail. I went to the local library, every school teacher and village mother; finally I had quite a list compiled. I typed them up and read off a different village each week. If I heard of a child in the hospital, having a birthday or a child visiting the island I would add this in my Magic Mirror time.

I had to round up the stories I was to read from all of my friends with kids as well as the library. For the music and songs I dug about in every collection on the island. There wasn't too much in the way of what I needed at the station but once I had a few cassettes and had some sent from home I did fine. By the time I was through I had quite a weird and wonderful collection. The favourite – at least of the girls I worked with – was Burl Ives singing "I saw an old woman who swallowed a fly." I'd be in the studio taping and they would be convulsed in laughter in the control room. They were also sent into fits of laughter over some of my pronunciations of the Niuean names.

Some of the children on the Island.

I hadn't realized I was playing havoc with these names until one morning I went in to tape and Lofa came up and explained: "Betty, Premier Rex phoned me. He listens to your programs and thought you needed help with the pronunciation of some of the childrens' names." I don't know which surprised me more, the Premier listening to the programs (they were hardly sophisticated enough for an adult, especially Sir Robert himself) or how the names were really pronounced. I noticed a lot of words and names in Niuean have *n*'s in the pronunciation where none are in the written word. Anyway, with the help of Dorothy and Bertha the program ran the whole time we were there.

The radio program was great but it didn't take up much of my time, only two mornings a week so I was always trying to find something else to do.

I wanted to get into one of the villages and see village life. Friends of ours, Brian and Gail Gillespie and their two boys had successfully moved from the white settlement to a major village and were very much a part of it. I wanted a similar experience, but a small secluded village with just a few residents. I was grousing about the house one evening vocally wondering how to do achieve my desire when Bill said,

"For Petes sake Betsy – just go and visit one, why not Vaiea Village?"

"Vaiea – that's the vacant village by the farm. No one lives there!" I snorted.

"Vacant? I've workers who live there – Lisa, Lower Hutt."

Well, this was something new! I went to sleep that night with all sorts of plans floating about in my mind. By morning I had separated the good ideas from the ridiculous.

I would visit the village the next day taking some baking, hoping I'd have enough and see what developed. I set a huge batch of buns and baked six two-layer-cakes, iced them and cut them in half. I figured a half for each family would be fine. I wrapped them in tin foil and stuck them in the deep freeze to keep the ants out. The buns didn't burn and looked pretty good so I divided them up in separate bags.

By the time Bill got home from work I was weary in body but my spirit and enthusiasm was still on a high. I didn't tell a soul what I planned as I wanted to go by myself – a special private adventure.

By 8:30 next morning I was on the road, the back seat of my little car covered with bags of buns and layer cakes. I threw a sheet over it all in hopes the dust wouldn't sift through.

By the time I was halfway there I was started to get cold feet. What on earth would the people think! A strange Polagi wandering in with food at 10:00 in the morning wanting to be claimed like a waif. I think I might have turned back but for the thought of what I'd do with six cakes and dozens of buns. I didn't know the people, only the three girls who worked at the farm. But I carried on. I drove in and went to the house Bill said Lisa lived in. From the moment the car stopped people slipped out of what I thought were vacant homes and when Lisa came to the door I knew my hunch was right. This was my village and my people! I had enough of everything for each home, met the mothers and made grand plans for the future. It was the beginning of a lovely friendship.

Vaiea, of course, was a very small village and quite poor. The homes were basic with very little furniture but were spotless. After this initial visit I tried to make it out every two or three weeks and gradually even the shyest of the ladies was open and friendly.

The ladies decided they'd like to learn to crochet. I think there were only two hooks in the whole village so I found some in a little shop and dug out all my bits of yarn and bummed from all my neighbours. Being a novice at crocheting still I figured a plain baby blanket of double crochet I could handle. Two or three of the ladies couldn't speak English so there was much merriment as we worked – usually at my expense. Soon the whole village was crocheting blankets of all colours and hues and I had my next problem. If we kept this up I'd need more yarn. I wrote to the WUCS headquarters back home begging for yarn and received a wonderful box full. Of course we had other projects too. Once our minister's wife, Margaret, came with me. She had a whole kit of colours for liquid embroidery so we hemmed up some material and each lady drew her design and we spent a wonderful morning painting all sorts of designs.

We also made jam out of limes, passion fruit and Paw Paws. I boiled it in an old tub over an open flame. We had *just* enough for all and the older kids showed up just in time to lick out the pot. I had brought buns so we had tea right there, new jam and all. I never did find out if it set; it was all gone!

Several Niuean girls, including some who worked at the farm, were expecting babies so the mother-hen in me got clucking and I bought some fine cotton and made nighties. I wanted to make diapers also but there was no flannelette available. Finally, I found a forgotten pair of lime green flannelette sheets tucked back on a shelf. So I bought them and made diapers. For that season several little bottoms were encased in green diapers!

There was no social stigma concerning these pregnancies, in fact it is an age old custom for girls to have children before marriage. Pregnancy proved they were fertile. No man wanted an infertile wife – he wanted children! I didn't feel sorry for the babies for they were wanted and loved by all. There is a wonderful extended family unit on Niue. In fact I've seen young mothers pick up another's baby to nurse if the mother was busy. But the girls, some pregnant by fifteen, lose their paychecks, have all chances of further education squelched, and are limited to a life as a village Mama.

It didn't take me long to realize that Niueans can sport some pretty strange names! It seems a name can be created out of any little happening on or near the birth of a child.

Lisa had her baby boy when the German cruise ship *Europa* was in port and thus she named him. This really isn't too bad but another child was called *Tinope*, because his Dad found a tin of peas on the reef the morning he was born. Brian Nichols, the man who graciously kept my car on the *run,* and his Niuean wife Louise, had twin boys within their brood which they named after two planes, which had at one time landed on Niue, thus the names *Hercules* and *Orion. Lower Hutt* was also named after a town in New Zealand. There was *Sincerely Yours* and a *Yours Truly* on the island, also a *Holliday* and *Young Vivian.* There were also cases of hero worship – *Gary Cooper, John Wayne*, being examples.

They also had a habit of changing their names. Bruce used to check with each of his students what their names were to be for that semester.

Flora, Fauna and Little Creatures

The island of Niue is not a soft fairyland but is rustic, very beautiful, and unique. There are the beautiful flowers, typical of tropical islands. At times you would be driving beneath scarlet coloured arbors of the magnificent "Flame Tree," and the sky would be completely hidden and the crimson petals would cover the road.

The seed pods made marvelous kindling when dried and I would pick them and store them for the purpose. Each pod would be over a foot long and when dry were extremely hard and brittle.

There were all colours of Bougainvillea. We had one by our front patio which I had to cut back each month or I'd get speared with the thorns from it as I passed. All colours of Hibiscus grew profusely as did the Frangipani. Frangipani is the favoured of all flowers for making the traditional leis all the islands are so fond of. I'm sure there wasn't an islander coming or going sent off without leis of Frangipani. There were many other wild flowers, some blooming for only a short spell. One time I was going downtown and happened to glance off to the side to see a whole vacant lot covered in tiny pink flowers, a complete mat of them. They were about as high as our Prairie Crocus and were bell shaped. I never found out what they were. The natives regarded them as weeds, but to me they were magnificent.

And of course the coconut palms, Tui told me there are over one hundred ways a coconut palm can be used. It's the "life blood" of the island. The wood makes furniture, pleated leaves made baskets, hats, carpets, partitions and shelter for festivities. A silky lace like growth near the crown yields good mats. The heart of the palm makes excellent salad. The husk can be used for insulation and the hard shell, charcoal. The liquid inside is delicious for a drink and is so sterile it has been used as a saline solution. As for the meat its uses are many. On the island few nuts are allowed to ripen into the coconut we buy in the market. If they do ripen the milk is useless to drink.

Some are made into copra for their oil which is used for soap and margarine. Most however, are picked young when the meat is soft and can be eaten with a spoon. A lot is used in coconut cream which Niueans use a great deal in their cooking. It is the "spice" of Niuean cooking – the added touch.

Bananas grow well on Niue. Even during the terrible drought there would be bananas. The rain forest was full of all the tropical plants. Creepers which we pay forty dollars for here grow profusely, at first I was dazzled remembering how I bought them at home for a great price then marvelled if it grew a new leaf and grumbled when it inevitably died. I would wander into the bush just gazing but in a few months I was slashing away at them like a Niuean.

Niue has few creatures, far fewer then most tropical countries. Any they do have are more of a nuisance than a danger. The ones that bugged me the most were the tiny sugar ants. These pests, hidden away in cracks and crevices, would appear like magic if you left an almost invisible crumb of food on a counter. You'd wipe it clean but when your back was turned there would be this string of little ants about an inch wide over to the crumb and back. Heaven forbid if you left out the bread and some other food stuff. I could hardly cool a cake before they'd show up and there were times when they beat me to it. At first it bothered me but soon I was just giving a good blow and what didn't lift off we ate. That's the unwritten law if you hope to maintain your sanity.

I used cans of DDT which I'd spray in all cracks and crevices, but you just couldn't get them all. In the wet season of course, they and indeed all the insects were worse. The ants which were the most destructive were tiny but had large black heads. These ones ate your underwear!

You couldn't leave any clothes, especially clothes with polyester or nylon in them on the floor as these ants would attack them and leave holes. I had nylon lounging pyjamas which were perfect for some of the grand affairs we attended and I took great care in the washing and ironing of them but it wasn't long before I noticed little holes. At first glance I thought of moths but I had never seen a moth that hungry! They were soon looking a bit like a sponge and I had to dump them. Most of us kept a pail of water handy and at night or after a shower we would pop our clothes into it. Still Bill's socks and my curtains were patterned with little holes.

There were cockroaches, big healthy ones one to one and a half inches long which came out at night. I had read somewhere that cockroaches can't stand candle wax so I bought a dozen cheap white candles and went to work rubbing every crack – the joints in drawers, all around the baseboards, the window sills, everywhere. It took me two days of hard labour. The last crack rubbed full of wax I washed up and went over to Tui's for a cold drink. "I'm done. I won't have a cockroach in the place," I said. Tui, being an islander, just looked at me in wonderment, a look I got many times from her wise eyes. "Don't be too sure Betsy," she replied. Sure enough, I got up that night and stood right on a huge cockroach! However, with spray and lots of scrubbing they were kept at a minimum.

My one cupboard was screened in and had the legs stuck in cans of kerosene so I could store some food stuffs in it. The rest had to be kept in the fridge and heaven help you if you left garbage by the stove. The house nearly walked away.

We also had lots of little geckos, lizards that walk on the ceilings and wall. they ranged from two to five inches long. They didn't bother me at all, but if one fell down my blouse or into the soup that was another matter. These little fellows ate the insects, or at least some of them and were interesting. You could hear them squeaking at each other at night as they flitted across the ceilings.

Once I had set a shallow bowl of icing sugar out and found

I was out of margarine so I hurried next door to get some from Annette. I ran there and back, however when I returned, there was a little gecko with its front feet on the edge of the bowl darting his tongue into the icing – in and out, in and out like a little kid would or kitten licking its milk from a saucer. The little creature looked almost human!

These little geckos were charming fellows!

The legend is geckos will never stay in an unhappy home. Well, we must have been absolutely deliriously happy because we had millions of them. I told Bill they must have liked my Irish Rovers tapes, but he figured not even a gecko would be that stupid.

When the rainy season arrived, little black millipedes did too. They are about one and a half inches long and quite harmless, but we also had some centipedes. I had heard stories of these creatures, none of which thrilled me. I was told by Niuean friends that they never had centipedes on the island until the Top Club was built and they had come in on the lumber used in the construction.

Jim Butler told me he had been bitten and it wasn't pleasant. The bite is dreadful and the after-effects are headaches, pains in muscles and even hallucinations. The only thing to do is take two strong Aspirin and rest. Bob Pope, a cabinet maker, had one in his shop in a jar and it fascinated me. We were in our little house for several months without a sign of one, then they moved in with all their kin.

I was cleaning out the spare closet and lifted a shoe to see if it was growing mold yet and just as I got it halfway up this thing leapt out of it, nearly scaring me to death.

But soon they were popping out of all sorts of strange spots. They can move extremely quickly. In just a second they can cover a great length of the room. Someone told me if a centipede is cornered it will actually take a run at you.

They are also really hard to kill. I'd whack away at them until they should have been mush, but still they'd wiggle away. One evening we were sitting in our front room visiting and I glanced up to see a huge centipede crawling out of a little hole in the corner, between the wall and the ceiling. I yelled and Bill got a stick and started demolishing it with me instructing him to really kill it or it would get away. There was only a blob left when he got through so we settled back. Fifteen minutes later I glanced over and lo and behold there was the centipede crawling down! I, in true fashion, had to inform Bill; "I told you they were hard to kill – there it goes!"

But on second look the first one was still a blob and this must have been its mate.

Neither of us were bitten by an adult centipede but one evening we were up at Bruce and Eileen's and I was chatting in the kitchen when I felt a real sting on top of my instep. I thought it was a wasp but upon closer inspection there was a tiny centipede sliding off my foot. It stung for a few minutes then I forgot all about it. That night, however, I had the most dreadful nightmares and woke up feeling dizzy and disoriented. I'm not sure if the venom was strong enough in such a little one to cause these symptoms or if it was simply mind over matter. It some how sounds more adventurous to claim I've been bitten by a centipede!

We also had moths. Some were so tiny they could come through the window screens. These ones were a nuisance, especially in the hot humid weather. Every evening they would be drawn by the light and fly in by the thousands. The only way to keep them out was to sit in the dark. They would fly about and fall on the floor, but the little ants would arrive in the night and eat them up or haul them away.

The large moths were a different story, large ones the size of a tablespoon would come in clouds once a year and completely cover all the outside screens. In the morning they had to be swept into two or three garbage bags. I often wonder if any lived and flew away.

Of course, what island would be complete without spiders and we had prize winners.

The ones we know as Daddy Long Legs were in every corner. You could sweep the webs out of all the corners one morning and the next morning they'd be built up again. It was a daily chore, like making the bed.

The spiders I found unique were completely harmless but huge, easily covering a saucer and some big enough to cover a breakfast plate when their legs were stretched out. Our toilet area was small – just about six inches space between the walls. One day I was on the "throne" and I glanced at the wall. There was this huge spider. I hurried, believe me, but since the spider fascinated me I stood back and gazed upon it in wonder. It stayed on to become a part of the household much like a pet would. I named it Charles as it reminded me of Prince Charles – cute in a weird way.

The outside spiders were smaller but you should have seen the webs they would spin! They were beautiful just like lace. They were also extremely tough, however; not like the fine gossamer ones we know. If you had to separate these ones you couldn't just sweep them away. You literally had to cut them with sharp scissors or a knife. But they were magnificent, especially with dew drops on them.

There were no land snakes on Niue but there were many sea snakes and when the tide was in I'd see them in some of the pools. Some were poisonous I was told and Jim, who was always exploring, came very close to putting his hand right on a couple which were sunning on a coral outcrop he was climbing.

The pest that caused the biggest uproar in our happy home was the rat! I knew there were rats on the island and I had seen one or two in my travels. They were not as big as our Norway rat but bigger than a mouse. I had heard them crawling around in our attic but that was it. Then we had to have some workmen come to fix the hot water pipes and to do this they had to cut a hole in the ceiling. They patched it up haphazardly and I forgot about it.

First thing I knew we heard very suspicious sounding noises in the kitchen. Bill checked, nothing. The next night even more noise. We had rats! Now I'm not fond of rodents of any kind but I can keep my cool, Bill is another story! From time immemorial the Kilgour-MacKenzie clan have had a mouse phobia. Not a quiet shaky phobia, but a full blown screeching, climbing on the table phobia – men and women. Now Bill could stop a charging elephant, but show him a mouse!

I was told ,next morning, "Bets get rid of those rats!" in a tone I wasn't sure I liked. I phoned Henry at Public Works, "Please send your men back to repair this hole!" I stuffed the cracks full of old gunny sacking and went downtown and bought two rat traps. I've got them now, I figured, as I set the traps. Sure enough, one trap went in the night. I was sure my problem was solved. Oh, the dreams of the foolish.

I was pulling a drawer out from under the day bed and I saw what I thought was a lovely golden lizard – long and shiny. I figured I didn't really want a lizard under the day bed so I sprayed a quarter of a can of fly spray in the drawer and shut it, thinking I'd dig it out when it succumbed. What I didn't know was I had given a rats tail a slug of DDT. Next day I found the rats had chewed up the gunny sacking. Bill stated: "If the rats stay I'm going to the hotel."

"Fine," I thought, "you go can go farther than that if you like! "

I, however, did phone Henry. "Henry, I've got rats coming out of my ears and I'm about to lose my wedded spouse!"

Henry came, patched the hole and I caught two more rats. After a long and profuse apology I let Bill back into home and hearth.

Unlike some islands, we didn't have a fly problem, but what we did have to watch were hornets. They would build their nests in the bushes or under the eves and if disturbed look out. Bill had to burn at least three nests and if we heard a real shrill cry of pain from a child, three to one he had been bitten. We would run out with a package of frozen peas to lay over the sting. (The peas being loose in the bag seem to cover the sting better than an ice cube.) I was bitten only once and that should last me a life time.

Tui and I had been out in the rain forest picking mangos. There were two or three little kids dragging along and they were shinnying up trees to shake down the mangos. We were all in high spirits, laughing and talking but just as I was blazing the trail through some bushes to the next tree I shook up a nest of hornets. Within seconds my thigh was stung nine or ten times and it hurt so much I was screeching and jumping up and down. The only thing which helps is ice and we were a long way from home. I drove home with one hand while I rubbed my sore leg with the other, moaning all the way. The ice helped a bit and even though it was still very swollen the next day it didn't hurt. I learned my lesson – never charge through a bush!

Pass the Flying Fox Please!

No one ever went hungry on Niue. Some people possibly suffered from poor nutrition but there was always food of some sort available.

The island itself provided well for its inhabitants although a lot of these were seasonal of course. The coconut was always available and there were bananas, breadfruit, mangos and tapioca. The breadfruit is about the size of a grapefruit with bumpy green skin. The green skin peeled off and when sliced you could fry it in butter, marinate it, or bake it. A lot of the food was imported with a boat coming in once a month. Often supplies might run out, sugar, margarine, oil and if the boat missed a month due to a storm, a strike or even if the skipper decided to do a bit of fishing, then we would run out of some goods but other than that we had little problems.

The ladies of the island had an "open air" fruit and vegetable market every Friday morning. In the rainy season it was great but you had to be down there by 5:30 or 6:00 or everything would be well picked over.

Many of our Niuean friends would keep us supplied with fruits. I'd come home to find a whole bunch of ripe bananas on my door step and often when Bill arrived home he'd be loaded with paw paws and mangos, gifts from his workers. I loved paw paws. Not too sweet but with a distinct flavor. Usually eaten fresh but you can also bake them. Then pour in coconut cream and eat from the shell – just like peaches and cream.

Another exciting day for us was the day the boat arrived with supplies. By this time each month the shelves would be bare and our meals a bit frugal. The island took on a festive air, the liquor store would be closed during the ship's stay in Alofi Bay. It's said to discourage the workers from drinking while working the ship, true or not I'm not sure.

All the freight had to be brought in by liter (a raft-like structure) as there is no harbour. It takes a day or two to move the freight and unpack it so it was usually the second day before the food stuffs started to appear on the shelves. The three main stores usually brought in fresh produce which everyone craves. The island provides exotic fruits like paw paw, bananas and mangos but the thrill of all is to be able to buy an apple from New Zealand.

Tui, Rosie and I would get up and hustle like crazy to get to the stores, hitting every one of them, and purchasing enough to fill our larders once more; stocking up on sugar, cooking oil and all staples. The excitement simmered down a bit towards the end of a week but we would still visit all stores to see what new dry goods were available and buy the new island prints. Once in awhile we'd find something really neat like a new hard soap or talcum powder but these were luxuries we didn't often see.

Nearly all the food stuffs were imported from New Zealand and some of these were different from what I was used to and often the same things had different names. Our ketchup was tomato sauce, beets were beetroot, bottled drink was squash etc. Many items were completely alien to me and some were hard to get used to, such as canned lambs tongue. Now I had often cooked a beef tongue and peeled it with no questions but one time I was out of meat for Bill's sandwiches and the only thing available in town was lamb's tongue. I don't know what I expected but when I opened the tin there they were in all their glory. They looked like a human tongue to me but beggers can't be choosers so I stuck them between bread and lettuce with a shot of pepper and sent them off. Bill thought they were great but then he can eat blood sausages without any qualms!

The cuts of meats were very different too. The farm had a good slaughterhouse with a cooler and butchered a cow or two once a week for local consumption. Now I'm used to round steak and T-bone, roasts and stew meat. But they had silver side, top side, and fillets so I didn't know what I had or what to do with it!

Probably the most common imported meat was Pacific Corned Beef. It was as much a part of the island as coconut trees. This corned beef was of excellent quality, much better than what is available in Canada and could be bought in every size tin from a two serving to a huge can.

There was lots of meat to be sure, some strange I'll admit but one thing there wasn't was fresh milk. I was told there had been one attempt at dairying. Holstein cows were brought in and everything. But it all fell to the wayside. The routine of milking cows morning and night at set hours, seven times a week played havoc with the free and easy Polynesian lifestyle. Or perhaps played havoc with the cows! So the scheme was abandoned, much to the relief of the milkers!

There, however, was an excellent quality powdered whole milk product from New Zealand called Anchor Brand. It was the very best powdered milk I've ever found. I only wish it was available in Alberta.

A favourite dish was raw fish. Now I know that sounds awful but it really isn't raw. The fish was boned and cut in small pieces and marinated in lime juice for hours. Then it is squeezed out and mixed with coconut cream, sometimes a few onions are added. This dish shows up at every celebration. When I had guests in for high tea, I modified this recipe. I bought fresh or frozen mussels and marinated them all day in lime juice. Then I'd squeeze them out cut them in fine pieces, add a bit of mayonnaise, a few onions, and a dash of tomato sauce and serve on lettuce like a shrimp cocktail. It was delicious!

You'd think fish would be easy to buy, but you had to know a fisherman or place an order with one to get fresh fish. It was hard work and everyone needed their catch to feed their own families.

The biggest delicacy and the one that whets the taste buds of all islanders is a meal of "Flying Foxes." Flying Foxes are nothing more than bats. Their peculiar elongated snout and upright ears inspired the name. They can be found throughout the Pacific as well as on several continents. They live on fruits as well as the nectar from flowers. Conservationists tell us they are an endangered species and they are very vital to the regeneration of forests. But fruit farmers find them to be crop destroying pests. The ones on Niue were hunted by all the men with great skill and tenacity. One shot gun blast could kill many at a time and I know I wouldn't want to be a bat on Niue with a native hungry and in need of meat!

These bats were cooked in the Umu after the fur was singed off, rather like the down burned off a duck. Then if you were the lucky, or unlucky, which ever way you look at it, one was set on your plate, wings, teeth and all. I never ate one, not that I know of anyway and if I did it was well camouflaged.

Mary Magatogia, a New Zealander, and her Niuean husband, a teacher, caught one for a pet and kept it in a cage outside the back door. The first thing I noticed about it was the smell. They certainly kept the cage clean but it smelled like the rodent cages in the Calgary Zoo. They would take it out of the cage and it would hang from their thumb and look about and even sip juice from a teaspoon. A lot of people thought it was darling but bats and I never did get along. The most I could say was it certainly was interesting!

My very, very favourite treat on Niue was a good meal of land crabs. These crabs sometimes known as robber crabs or coconut crabs are huge with a heart-shaped body, gigantic claws and a great tail curled up beneath it. Its claws are quite capable of crushing a lead pencil or your finger if you are fool enough to give it a chance. These crabs are related to the little hermit crabs but have adapted themselves to life on dry land and only return to the sea for breeding. Real pests on coconut plantations they climb the palms, cut down some coconuts and then descend to rip off the husks from the fallen nuts and break them open with their great claws to feast on the soft flesh inside. They feed only at night and so it is at night they are hunted. A coconut is cut open with just a small hole to give limited access to the coconut flesh inside. The nut itself is attached to some anchor point like a big rock or tree root. Then you hide and grab the crab while it's trying to get at the coconut flesh.

The first time I ever saw one of these creatures was one evening Young Sefo, a worker from the farm, brought me two of them in a gunny sack. Of course they were still alive. I thanked him profusely and asked him to please dispatch them before he left but he just laughed and said, "No Mama, you must cook them alive! They will wait until tomorrow." and off he went whistling away. I eyed that sack with a good bit of trepidation as I gingerly lifted it over and set it beside the little chip heater. Bill was in bed sound asleep so I couldn't ask him if the creatures would know enough to stay in the sack. I turned out the lights and went off to bed. In the middle of the night I heard this clunk, clunk clunk.

"O, brother, they're out!", I didn't want to wake Bill as he has a dreadful time getting back to sleep if he wakes in the night and he had to be off early each morning. So I gingerly crawled out, expecting to lose a toe or two at any moment. I got to the bedroom light okay, then the hall. When I finally peered into the front room there was the sack with the crabs still inside. They had just taken a stroll, sack and all. I didn't take any chances however. I moved the sack into the spare room closed the door and locked it!

I had never cooked a crab in my life so I went over to Tui's to see if she knew what the procedure was. We decided on the spot we'd have a great dinner that night and invite Rosie and Godfrey and boys. We cooked up a storm all day. We put a great pot of water on to boil and when it was ready we opened the sack. Neither Tui nor I wanted to reach in and grab the creatures so she held one side of the sack and I the other and we shook the poor things out. That night we broke them apart with a heavy knife handle and dug the meat out and dipped it in melted butter. My it was delicious! Every chance thereafter I ate crab, so much so it was known throughout the island that Mama Betty loved the coconut crab. The week before we left to come home Olive came bringing gifts, one being a parcel of twelve cooked land crabs to "take home to Canada Betsy!"

Families kept both pigs and chickens. Many villagers had a pig or two and even the whites built little shelters and fattened baby pigs they had bought through the Agricultural Department. I love keeping chickens and pigs but Bill wanted nothing but the lawn out back. He remembered all to vividly years ago, having to crawl under a tractor to repair something only to find his back covered in oozy green chicken droppings:

"No chickens and no damn pigs either Bets!"

So I used to save my leftovers and peelings for one of our friend's pigs. Still it was always in the back of my mind — I'd love a pig to raise.

We had friends in Canada who were planning on visiting us. Lucy had won a trip to Rarotonga and I had it all mapped out. When Stan and Lucy visit us I'll have Stan build me a pig house when Bill's at work. Bill won't yell too much in front of friends and by the time they leave he'll have cooled off. Besides I could handle a bit of "hot tongue and cold shoulder" if I got a couple of good pork roasts out of it all. But Stan and Lucy didn't come. Some bright travel agent in Calgary informed them it would cost $2,000 to fly to Niue from Rarotonga instead of $200. Of course by the time they got to Rarotonga it was too late to make connections so there went my pig house. But I don't give up easily.

About halfway through our stint Tui and I decided we would each get a little feeder and keep them at her place. She had a pen of sorts and I had lots of peelings. We put in our order and waited in great expectation. The day they arrived we threw a B.B.Q. to celebrate, only noone knew why. Anyway, we pampered the little darlings like you wouldn't believe. We fed them two or three times a day and checked them forty. But within a month's time one looked a bit ill so we fed it more but the next week one was down right sick and the other's ears were drooping. We asked the pig man what was wrong and he said we had over fed them to such a degree they'd never recover. We had killed them with kindness. We got a few chops of the poor critters but that was the end our pig enterprise.

Next to pork, chicken is my favourite meat. The ocean was full of fish and the deep freeze full of beef but I wanted chicken. Bill said, "Bets, if we lived on a chicken ranch you'd want fish!" There were lots of wild chickens clucking about the island and even our settlement. So Tui and I devised a scheme. We would trap some for the freezer. I found a big wooden crate about 3' by 3' and we propped it up on one end with a stick to which we tied a cord and sprinkled some rice under the box. Then we waited until late afternoon when the chickens came pecking. Tui watched out my kitchen window

CLUCK?

and I held the cord. When a poor chicken wandered under the box She would yell "Now," and I'd give the cord a pull. Down came the box and we had our chicken! We took turns reaching in and holding them while the other chopped its head off with a bush knife. We caught quite a few this way. They were not that good however, tough and stringy, but it was the trapping that was the fun and the challenge.

One day we caught five, Tui took two and I took three. There was a party we had to attend that night and time was too short to clean and pluck them but if I left them they'd spoil so I poked them in a garbage bag and tossed them in the deep freeze, feather, guts and all. When we got to the party Tui asked,

"Did you get you chickens cleaned Betsy?"

"They are in the freezer Tui!" I replied, not mentioning in what condition.

When I dug them out next morning and partially thawed them the feathers came out far easier then the old way. I had hoped to finish the job and have them back in the deep freeze before Tui came over but she caught me red handed. I doubt I'll ever live that one down. I still say I found it a far easier way to pluck chickens.

The prison was just behind the Top Club and the inmates had a wonderful vegetable garden so Tui, Rosie and I would drive over and buy vegetables when they were available.

Anytime I felt compelled to make pickles I'd scoot over to see what the prisoners had growing. I always managed to get enough variety, although some of my combinations were weird to say the least. I became sort of a "Jailbird Jenny" and was treated royally. Maybe, because I'd take a jar over for them to taste after each pickling session.

One time Tui, Rosie and I stopped by and I started chatting with one fellow. He was friendly and showed me the garden. I started to ask him what he was in for but Tui kicked my ankle and dragged me off. With my over active imagination I immediately thought it must be something really dreadful. Otherwise why would Tui try to keep me from finding out! When we were safely out and away I asked her what the kick was about. She replied, "Betsy! That man was the Warden!"

There were pumpkins growing on the island, started by someone years ago, but these are different than the ones I knew. They have a very tough skin and many times I used the axe to chop them in half and quarters. The inside was also firmer, more like our squash. I saw them in a magazine when we arrived home and learned they are called winter pumpkin.

I used it as a dessert base much to the utter amazement of all my friends, Polagi and Niuean. I remember making pumpkin pie, I served it to Jacob and his wife Vaeola, but decided not to enlighten them as to its contents. They polished off one whole pie but when I told them what it was made of they wouldn't believe me. They were adamant, pumpkin it was not. It was the same story when I served pumpkin cake for the first time.

We always had food and enough shortages to be interesting but not enough to cause hardship in my eyes, but in some other's eyes it was totally different.

One day I was in K mart and two ladies came in. K mart had just received a great shipment of potatoes and we were all buying some. I overheard the mother-in-law lament in a very doleful manner to her daughter-in-law, "You'd better get two or three sacks. You never know when you'll see them again in this Godforsaken hole!"

Visitors to the Island

Before we left on the posting we were asked by all and sundry "Won't you feel cramped and trapped on an island that small? Only two planes a week and a boat once a month?" Well, the island is small to be sure but I couldn't help but think, rather drily, there are many times on our farm when the cattle got off the place more often than I did, so I couldn't believe I'd be too bothered. Bill on the other hand is a different story, if he has his work, three squares a day and a good conversationalist to chat with over a coffee he'd live happily in a packing crate.

From the time we arrived until our departure neither of us ever felt trapped. Our home was always full of a great variety of friends and when it wasn't we could go and visit them or partake in any number of hobbies or projects. If I felt a twinge of cabin fever I could take off in my car and believe me in that car if I went five miles it felt like fifty!

Of course the day of the mail plane was the highlight of the week and was awaited in eager anticipation not to mention cramped and callused fingers from keeping up with all the correspondence we needed to have written, stamped and in the Post Office by noon of *The Day*. At home I get the mail every morning and it's no big deal but try receiving mail only once a week! It turns the whole procedure into a very special holiday – a bit like Christmas and only slightly lower than my wedding! The plane usually arrived about 4:00 p.m. and the mail bags would be hustled down to the Post Office for sorting. This would be completed by 6:00 or 6:30 p.m. We'd wait with baited breath and much clock watching. Then Bill and Barry would tear down for the mail. One point in favour of once a week mail — you got a good pile and it was so precious. Even the newspapers a month old were read with great excitement. Especially the one from your own hometown. But if for some reason the plane was late, or heaven forbid, didn't arrive at all, it was like a cloud of doom arrived in its place.

The odd time someone really special would arrive. One example is the Queen of Tonga. I had read of the Queen for years, remembering the news flashes when she attended Queen Elizabeth's coronation, so I was there with the rest of them to view this new royal personage. Our own Lady Patricia was there, so royal herself as she curtsied the Queen. I was surprised the Queen was so short. I had always read of the Tongan race being tall, big, and majestic so I figured she being the Queen, should be taller, bigger and more majestic! She was majestic but short!

But the most exciting arrival was that of Prince Edward, Queen Elizabeth's youngest son. He was teaching at a boys private secondary school at Wanganui (collegiate) in New Zealand at the the time and he was taking a break to visit some islands. The whole island was in the throes of excitement for weeks. Every village was out in full force picking up junk and trimming hedges. Alofi was scrubbed, painted and shone like a new penny. Prince Edward was to spend two days, I believe, but what a two days. He was to be wined and dined and entertained with as many islanders as possible included in the many events. The girls at the radio station were all excited and for weeks talked of nothing else.

"Hey, maybe he will ask me for a date!" Bertha giggled.

"Not when he sees me," Lofa replied.

The room exploded with laughter, however, when I declared, "He's all yours *after* I'm through with him!"

He stayed at the New Zealand Residency with Jane and Malcolm, in fact he slept in their bed. The second evening Bill and I were really fortunate to be invited to a grand open-air High Tea at the Premier's house.

The guests sat on benches and chairs in front of the verandah of the house to listen to the speeches of welcome and the words from a honest to goodness prince! Mrs. Rex gave a lovely speech finishing it with a flourish as she asked the Prince if she could impart a motherly kiss on his princely cheek. He agreed.

After his own short eloquent speech, Malcolm toured him through the guests introducing him to several. He was accompanied by his companion – sort of a male lady-in-waiting. Also several big policemen were watching one and all very closely. He stopped to chat with Bill when Malcolm explained we were from Canada. It rather amazed him to find a person from Canada so far from home. As Malcolm toured the princely guest through a large group of Niuean Mamas, they were not in the least awed but rather chatted away like happy golden birds, teasing the prince. One of them cut loose and grabbed Malcolm's arm and proceeded to place wet kisses from hand all the way to his elbow in great smacks, but Malcolm was unflappable as usual, forever the gentleman.

The Prince also spent an evening dancing at the hotel. The word was he was very friendly and danced happily with all the golden beauties, but of course that wouldn't be too much of a hardship.

The next time I saw the girls at the office I was anxious to hear what they thought of the visitor.

"Betty, he's just a little boy!"

And indeed he looked like a young fresh faced eighteen-year-old which is exactly what he was!

A German Cruise ship caused a stir in Niue when it arrived one day. The little island was overrun with tourists, in the strangest get-ups from high rubber boots to parkas with cameras strung around their necks, clicking away at anything and everything that caught their eye. They wanted lots of keepsakes like the fine weaving but groused about the price, haggling away with the shop girls. But of course they probably needed their money to pay for the trip.

The Niueans were always extremely kind to all the tourists, showed them a great time but they had the good humour to chuckle at some of them and their manner. The funny thing was, I was chuckling right along with my friends, forgetting I was a Polagi. The girls at the office treated me as a Niuean though I remember foolishly staying out in the sun longer than was wise once and got a dilly of a sunburn on my shoulders. Bertha and Dorothy met me on the street and in no uncertain terms scolded me, "Betty you're acting like a Polagi, allowing yourself to burn – smarten up!"

Niue had a New Zealander, Brian and Margaret Sayer launch Niue Adventures. Brian, a highly qualified scuba diving instructor, was able to qualify a student in three different ratings, and introduce his students to the underwater world around Niue. In fact divers came from all over the world for the very clear, perfect diving opportunities on the island. While Brian was there he had a bit of trouble with pilfering on his boat but he unwisely wrote a scalding letter to the editor about this, rebuking the people, stating how he came to help the island and they repaid him by stealing! He must have written it in anger as he was normally a peaceful man.

A week or so later his yacht sank in the harbour. Of course the coconut telegraph was burning with the story and it was figured that the caustic letter was the cause of it all and the ship was sabotaged! But when the air cleared Brian explained a rope had slipped – it was his own fault. I notice, however, the islanders worked right along with the Polagis to bring the ill-fated *Extravagance* up once more.

One other visitor I remember was Paul Falconer from Queensland. He arrived to try our waters for scuba diving, staying five days. He traveled light but his pride and joy was a really good spear gun which he had borrowed from a friend. It was too long to tuck inside his luggage so he tied it to the handle. As soon as he landed it was spotted by the Niueans and the battle of wits ensued.

It disappeared from the bag immediately, going through customs, so when Paul picked up his bag – no spear gun. He fussed and fumed and voila there it was – it had fallen off somehow!!

Several times during his stay this prize was admired, gazed upon and generally coveted and he told us all about it. So as he packed to leave he made his mind up – no one was going to touch it. He had to tie it to the bag once more as he wasn't allowed to carry it aboard but he watched it being lifted into the baggage compartment. Thinking he won in the end he finally boarded and the plane took off. But guess what! As Barry came down from the control tower he noticed the spear gun clutched in a hand on its way to its new home. Barry stopped the fellow,

"That's Paul's spear gun – how did you get it?"

"Oh, he sold it to me," was the reply.

I can just imagine Paul's chagrin when he arrived home – he had lost the battle of wits, or rather the battle of the spear gun.

Incidence of serious crime and violence is extremely low on Niue. However, there was the incident of August 14, 1953 when the Resident Commissioner, Mr. Larsen was murdered in the night and his wife assaulted by three escaped prisoners who seemed to have a personal vendetta against Mr. Larsen for his harsh treatment.

Mr. Larsen was a very forceful man with ideas and vision ahead of his time but his manner on implementing these caused much strife and pain. Still his murder threw a black cloud over the island as well as New Zealand for some time. The very small population of the island and the close compact nature of Niuean society serve to keep most antisocial behavior within tight bounds. The only crime I ever noticed was the lifting of small items and the odd empty petrol tank. Our home was broken into one night while we were asleep. And, I thought I was a light sleeper!

Bill woke in the morning to find some panes out of the window and realized what had happened. We lost sheets, my radio, Bill's dress pants, food and money from Bill's wallet.

They had carried the pants to the kitchen and cleaned out the wallet, leaving the Canadian money. Then they emptied the potatoes and used the sack for the loot. What bothered me the most was my feeling of helplessness. That people could come into my house and I could do nothing about it. But I know that this happens all the time in Canada, often with brutality thrown in, and in all other countries as well. It's just more obvious on a small island. I never once was afraid on Niue and I knew if I had trouble I would have had help in a minute.

The odd time the Calibration Plane landed and if you knew the time, were a friend of the pilot or Barry and more important the plane had a vacant seat, you could catch a ride to Rarotonga. These were government planes and would be flying to the various islands on business.

Once in awhile a passenger jet would, for some reason or another, usually due to a break down of something, be forced to stay over. This could cause a stir. The hotel holds forty and the Hinemata Motel only has three rooms and if the plane was full which it usually was, there would be people needing a place to lay their weary heads. When this happened the powers that be would call on us at Fualahi – each home would be asked to take a passenger or two. The one time it happened when we were there we played host to a middle aged fellow from Las Vegas who reminded me of Ricardo Monteban minus the accent.

Many of our peers had visitors from their homeland during their stay on the island. It was lovely for them, mothers and fathers, and siblings and other relatives would arrive for a week or two and we'd all meet and enjoy them.

Bill and I, being so far away didn't expect any kith or kin to come and see our island, but to our great surprise and greater thrill, near the end of our stay some friends from home, who were visiting relatives in Australia, decided to detour our way. We had known Gordon and Alice Park and their family all our married life and were good friends so we were delighted. The minute we received the great news we started planning. They would only be with us for five short days so we had to pack a lot into that time.

They had to see the caves, the reef and other natural sights. Gordon had to spend a day at the farm and Alice had to hit the shops with me. I scrubbed and baked and in the evenings we planned. We wanted them to meet all our friends, Niuean and Polagi, so we decided to have a buffet at the hotel for all. Then in order to give them a taste of island culture we would ask the Tongan dance group to perform after the meal. Bill's truck driver was William, a tall handsome Tongan. Bill approached him and it was all arranged. The day the plane was due Tui and I made leis out of frangipani and arranged more through our house. Gordon and Alice arrived and all went as planned.

Gordon and Alice Park, our only visitors from afar.

Socializing

Another wonderful facet of life on Niue was the social life. We had never lived such a social whirl in our entire lives and probably never will again.

Niue being such a unique island a person could mix with all walks of life, from the poorest villager to the Premier, from the girls who cleaned to the Resident Representatives wife, all special in their own way.

The most coveted invitation was the special engraved ones sent out from the Niue government or the Premier's desk. Every few months a dinner or party in honour of visiting dignitaries or a Constitution Celebration or any number of other occasions would be held at the "Fale Fono" or Government Building. We were fortunate enough to be invited to many of these celebrations. Of course most of the guests were Niuean; government officials, business men and women with a smattering of Polagis.

The waitresses for these events were local girls and their job was to circulate with drinks and snacks. However, instead of just walking they would creep along, crouching so their heads were about waist level. I was amazed when I saw this performance. I imagine it is a sign of respect but I doubt I could crouch and walk at the same time. I would be just a bit afraid I'd upend either myself or someone else!

For these occasions, especially the evening ones, I needed cocktail dresses or "after five" styles. Not needing a lot of these back home on the farm my closet was embarrassingly bare of suitable clothes. Of course there was no way to

purchase any so Tui, Rosie and I paid a visit to the local clothing factory. Miriam owned this business and had three or four
seamstresses hired and a minimum of fabric and the patterns
were old and tattered. I found some fine cotton crepe in white
and burnt orange. By this time I had a pretty fair tan so figured
both would look good. I found two patterns and combined
them for the white and picked one which boasted on bare
shouldered and low mid calf length for the orange. It was quite
a decision for the woman who lives in casuals and two piece
suits but it was also exciting. Rather like Cinderella in thongs,
only my carriage was a Morris Minor.

Several shops had colourful Island prints and each time a
new shipment would come in Rosie, Tui and I would buy
some. From these we made sundresses which were all one
could wear during the heat of the day. For evening B.B.Q.s
and entertaining I bought bright three yard lengths which
became very loose and casual Mu Mus.

Many times various social events would take place at the
Residence of the New Zealand representative. Everyone
enjoyed these as Jane and Malcolm were impeccable hosts
and the residence was by far the nicest, most elegant home on
the island.

But all our socializing wasn't confined to great government
functions and dinner parties. We also seemed to find ourselves
at B.B.Q.s at least once a week. The wonderful tropical evenings were perfect for barbequeing and nearly everyone in our
settlement had a B.B.Q. of some sort built in the backyard.
Usually Rosie, Tui and I worked together and held it at Barry
and Tui's.

We always mixed our groups, teachers, villagers, Irish,
Niuean, whatever – a real melting pot. Tui was a marvel at
planning a party. We used to make a punch, and I mean
punch, everything went into it, fruit juice, pop and a good dash
of gin and vodka.

I also found myself entertaining at home in a style I wasn't
used to. At home in Alberta we would have friends for Sunday
dinner at noon or possibly for supper at 6:00 but on Niue

entertaining was much more genteel or civilized. I had many guests for a casual lunch and even for breakfast but the real entertaining was an evening affair. I used to invite the guests to come at 7:00, planning on eating at 7:30. I thoroughly enjoyed entertaining and when I returned home found my old meat, potatoes and gravy at 6:00 dull indeed.

One guest I had invited for an afternoon cup of tea was Lady Rex. I decided I should give my little house an extra polish. I knew how curious a lady she was – one who would in all likelihood ask for a grand tour which in my house would take all of three minutes but I didn't want cobwebs or pig buckets about. It wasn't every day I got to entertain a Premier's wife. I worked like crazy – even cut out pictures of flowers, pasted them on coloured paper and stuck them up in the little toilet.

Annette and Eileen came early, each making treats to serve and helping dust what cups I had. None of us had really good china or silverware so I made do but I didn't want a dust ball from the cups I had to get lodged in Lady Rex's teeth.

I wore my best sundress and squeezed my sweaty, swollen feet into a pair of shoes.

All went great – but wouldn't you know it she never asked to see the house after all my fancy cleaning and decorating. I was terribly tempted to ask her if she'd like to use the toilet but I managed to control myself.

Eggs, Shells and Coral

I was seldom homesick probably because I kept so very busy that time sped by at an accelerated rate.

But the first Easter season I had a bout of depression. I missed the kids and the fun of the Easter Bunny. When I get depressed I can't stand myself so I dig myself out in self defense. This time I decided I'd have a special Easter Egg colouring party and invite all the kids in our settlement.

"Should be fun!" I thought. I bought eggs by the dozen, borrowed food colouring from friends to go along with my lone red one and found some felt pens. I made a pile of lacy doilies out of writing paper, folding each and everyone which way and cutting away in wild abandon.

Our Easter egg colouring – my feet hurt but
my "blues" were gone by the end of the day.

Next I took the tour of all the homes, inviting each child. Some children had never heard of the Easter Bunny – but they were excited. When the great day arrived I shoved all the furniture against the wall leaving the table free for kids to walk around. I lay out layers of newspaper on the floor. I boiled five dozen eggs, and mixed the colours in little margarine tubs. All was set and ready when the kids arrived. At first some kids were a bit shy but soon they were all having a sloshing good time.

Some of the children were very artistic and had lovely patterns, others, well, beauty is in the eye of the beholder. What a mad afternoon. Colours spilled over the table, eggs accidentally dropped, kids chattered away like magpies. It was 4:30 when I finally called a halt to the festivities and handed out ice cream cones and passion fruit juice. I think the biggest struggle was finding boxes and bags to to carry their treasures home in.

By the time I got everything cleaned up I was over whatever depression I had been in. All I wanted to do was sleep.

The Top Club was near our settlement and boasted a nine hole golf course. Bill and I are not golfers but I was asked to be one of the judges at their annual golf meet. Jane Russell, a new neighbour, Dr. Peter, a young doctor taking his tropical disease training on Niue and I were to judge the outfits of the competing teams. It was fun and as a thank you we each received a lovely bouquet of island grown Orchids. The first and last orchids I ever received.

The tennis court was always busy and Margaret Kong started a "Jane Fonda exercise class" three times a week. Margaret, a New Zealander, and was married to Lester Kong, the Resident Representative's Secretary. Lester was from Malaysia and they had two children. Tui and I were the oldest exercisers but could keep right up. However, my outfit left a bit to be desired! Most of the whites had the leotard and tight combinations in all sorts of colours but I wore my bathing suit with a baggy shirt over top. I didn't start a new trend. I guess I was just too avant garde for the times!

For me the joy of my life was shelling. As I've stated before, there is no sand beach on Niue, just coral cliffs which one had to climb down to get to the reef. I'd watch the tides closely and when I figured them out I'd head for the reef, plastic bag in hand. I went through many friends conning them into accompanying me. Eileen and I went together often. Eileen was a tender, soft spirited lady her lovely Irish side always obvious. But whereas I would grab any shell big or small alive or dead and think nothing of it, Eileen was so soft hearted she only picked empty shells not wanting to hurt any creature. If she noticed one of my shells crawling about my bag she'd beg me to put it back safely in the water. Once I noticed quite a good sized cowrie but just as my hand hit it she gasped "But Betty! It's a family member." Of course big mean me could take them home and boil them or put them in the deep freeze to kill the insides without a qualm, and Eileen knew this.

But while we were away on holidays Eileen went shelling. She told me the sad tale. While she was driving to her favourite spot she kept praying, "Please don't let me find a really big one! Please God." You see if she found a really big one and it was alive she would be severely tempted to keep it! You can imagine her mixture of horror and delight when in the first pool she looked there was the granddaddy of all – a huge cowrie shell. She did a lot of debating but finally decided she couldn't leave it but she would take it immediately to Gary and Sue's big aquarium. That way she would have her cake and eat it to – so to speak.

When we arrived home, we heard the news. It was a lovely shell – the biggest I had ever seen. I wish I could say it lived happily ever after but it succumbed in due time.

Tui and I often went shelling too. Tui being an island lady was very familiar with reefs and ocean and all its creatures so it was educational as well as fun when I shelled with her. One memorable time we were on the reef in the afternoon chatting away as we lazily looked in the little pools. All of the sudden

Tui noticed a movement on a rock at the edge of a pool. On investigation she realized it was an octopus. We found it hiding in a hole in the coral but Tui is not easily defeated.

Octopus is a delicacy and we were not going to lose this one. She ordered me to get a long stick and while she pounded in the crevice I pulled on a tentacle. The water turned a muddy purple as we worked away. It must have taken a good ten minutes before the creature let go and we had it. It was not a big one – the length from head to end of tentacles would be about three feet in all. We had pretty well demolished it with our pounding. We took pictures, giggling away about our fishing adventure and Tui cooked it up for supper. It wasn't that great a taste – rather like chewing on an old rubber boot but the conquest was exciting!

Many times I'd go shelling alone and these were my quiet times, the time to relax and think – a spiritual time. If the tide was out I'd get Bill off to work and leave for the reef. It was always so peaceful and soothing that time of day and I'd walk along, hunting for shells until the tide started in again. Then I'd head back to my busy day, replenished in soul and spirit.

At first I picked up every shell I found – five-year-old ones, fresh ones with creatures in them, broken ones, miniscule ones – everything. But after awhile, like 5,000 shells later, I became more particular and would keep only the special ones. My favourite shell is the cowrie, the bigger the better. At one of my shelling places I found many money cowrie which are still used as currency on some of the Solomon Islands.

Shelling is fun – especially the hunting but once home the work begins. It's a right smelly business. To kill the creatures inside you can either stick them in a plastic bag in the deep freeze overnight or you can dump them in boiling water for a half hour or so. Though you have to keep them in water mixture for days until all the insides come clean. In order to clean them you have to dig away with toothpicks and it takes time. Some shellers buried the shells and let the little ants eat it all up but I used the water method. I very often had two or three dishes of shells in various stinky conditions at one time but still the call of the reef would be so strong I'd go again for more.

The reef had to be treated with respect. It can only be walked on in sand shoes. Big waves can sweep in and knock a person flying when you least expect it and the sharp coral can deliver a severe cut.

Bill, Bruce and I were out one evening and I wandered close to the edge of the reef. I had my back to the ocean which is not wise and a gigantic wave was just waiting, and it swept in catching me behind the knees and down I went. I was scrambling about trying to grab onto a rock or something before the wave came back. I was sure I was going to be swept out to sea. I hung on for dear life as another wave caught me. Then all settled back. I was shaking all over I finally got up and walked towards the cliff. I felt no pain but when I glanced down I saw I my knee was bleeding profusely from a gash. I wiped it off and started shelling once more. I couldn't feel a thing and figured it was just a little scratch, but Bill and Bruce noticed it hadn't stopped bleeding and from his vantage point Bruce was sure it needed stitches.

We went home and I showered and tied a cloth about it and proceeded to make supper but the blood still had not clotted, so off to the hospital, where it took eight stitches to close it. You have to be very careful with a coral cut as it can infect quickly causing a very high fever with painful swelling if not checked with an anti-biotic.

Infection in tropical zones quickly turn into tropical ulcers and can take many weeks to heal. I saw one ulcer on a lady's leg, and she was having a terrible time with it as it wouldn't heal. It was huge, bigger than our fifty cent piece. The ulcer, even when healed, can leave a dreadful scar.

But I didn't go to the reef just to collect shells – there is a beauty there one wouldn't find anywhere. There are pools teaming with the most extravagant and colourful tropical fish, and pools full of coral of shades of colour which would take your breath away. I have never seen such colours, vivid blues, greens and pinks, no artist could imitate the patterns formed by underwater coral.

In my ignorance I decided to take some home. I took a hammer and proceeded to beat off branches of the various colours. I brought it home in a sack fully expecting it to stay the same but, of course, coral is a living organism and when broken off it dies, so all I had was a few branches of ugly grey dead matter. I did put it in bleach so at least it was white and to my eye now, quite lovely.

Bruce was an avid snorkeler and when we went out to the reef with him he'd talk Bill into trying his mask. It took a bit of coaxing but after a few times he was hooked. Brian and Bill would float about gazing at the fish while Eileen and I shelled. Bill felt funny at first, his face and hands tanned to leather but being as how he always wore long jeans there was a great length of white leg on show when he floated along, not unlike a great white shark on the prowl. There was a sports shop in Alofi and I tried to get Bill to buy himself a set of snorkel and flippers but he didn't want to commit himself. But one evening Tui and I ganged up on him literally and figuratively. We badgered him like two fox terriers until he, in desperation, took off and lo and behold came back with a set. He never regretted the purchase and even now when friends go on holiday to Hawaii he expands on the glory of snorkelling and lends his equipment to them.

For the real hearty of heart and body, there are wonderful places to visit, limestone caves grottos, chasms, some you have to play "Tarzan," rope and all to get to. One called the Key Hole is also hard work as you literally crawl through an opening only slightly larger than one.

Many of the caves, especially those inland, were used as burial places and human bones can still be found in them. The native people will not enter these as they feel the "aitu," or ghost, is still dwelling there. At Ana you can, with a guide, see the Japanese fishing vessel, the *Yashio Maru*, which was wrecked during a storm in 1967. Tuo is another interesting stretch of reef. It was here in ancient times mothers were permitted to throw unwanted children over the cliff. After making the proper incantations to the gods, of course.

Japanese fishing vessel wrecked in 1967.

Fish Stories

We had a neighbour in our settlement, Peter Robinson, who was an avid fisherman. Every day he could possibly get away he'd take his boat down to the dock and spend the morning fishing. We used to buy the odd fish from him, barracuda being the very best but also tuna. He'd take a friend with him now and again, always coming home with fish.

My fishing experience thus far was sitting on a bank dangling a hook in a quiet beaver pond but for some nutty reason I decided I wanted to try deep sea fishing! I finally got up the courage to ask Peter, hoping he didn't hold to any old superstition like "women cause storms" etc. He looked at me strangely – "Really!" as if he couldn't believe his ears.

"Yes, I promise I won't rock the boat or anything!"

"Okay next time I go but you have to get up early, we leave about 4:30 a.m."

I was ecstatic. I had visions of hooking and fighting a giant barracuda, for half an hour before finally pulling it in. I was so naive; I figured no one in their right mind would go out in a little motorboat unless the sea was calm.

Finally Peter came over.

"Ready to go fishing Betsy?!"

"Absolutely!"

So next morning I was up and over at Peter's by 4:20 and off we went – his partner Bob Skutz a New Zealander meeting us at the dock. The boat was lowered and into the water by the time it was daylight. I got in and received my instructions,

"Hold this line Betsy. If you feel a good tug start turning this crank."

I noticed life jackets under the seat and wondered if maybe I should put one on. The sides of the boat looked awfully low.

We were soon out in the ocean, but the waves; heavens, they were twelve feet high and we were in the trough. One of those babies could knock me over the edge in a second! Up and down we went. I wondered why on earth the men weren't afraid. I glanced over, Peter was whistling away and Bob was cleaning his nails. My hands were wrapped so tightly hanging on the knuckles were pure white and almost popping the skin. Still they just sat, I'm sure the waves were getting higher.

"Kinda rough this morning," I said, desperately trying to be nonchalant. "Maybe we should put on our life jackets."

Peter just glanced up, "We never bother with them when the sea is dead calm."

Dead calm I thought, I'd hate to be here in a storm!

After about a half an hour, I was having real trouble calming my panic. I was trying to figure out how to get back to shore without showing any fear. I finally figured I'd rather they think I was a landlubber who was seasick then one who was scared spitless. I tried to look green (which wasn't hard to do by this time) as I grabbed for a can and pretended I was about to upchuck my breakfast. I put on a real good act too.

Peter looked concerned and asked if I'd rather go ashore – I gasped, "Yes", giving a mighty spit in the can. On the way home he told me, "Lots of people get seasick – it's nothing to be ashamed of." I often wonder if Peter ever found out it had nothing to do with my stomach. It was my chicken liver that gave me the trouble.

The local men make their own outriggers called "vakas" out of local wood. "Moata" is the principal tree used for the hull. "Fou" is used for the outrigger and "Pili" is the glue used for caulking and comes from the "Al" tree. The fishermen are fearless, going out even during storms, and I saw them paddling away between the whales when the whale migration came by.

Local made outrigger.

I had a dream, not a monumental dream like Rev. Martin Luther King had – mine was a miniscule and completely selfish dream. I was determined to learn how to swim. This dream had been fermenting in the recesses of my brain for many years. As a child there was no way to learn, not even a regular bath tub for my first years, using instead a square galvanized tub. When I was older and was able to go to camp with the Canadian Girls in Training, I learned how to do the "Dead Man's Float," which I thought was a marvelous accomplishment. But still I wanted to swim. The dream was always there but there was little or no opportunity to learn.

On Niue I would watch Bill enjoying the water and the dream blew its cork and entered the forefront of my thoughts. I was petrified of the ocean, if I was going to learn I had to know I could stand if need be – preferably in five to six inches of water.

The hotel had a pool but I would have an audience there which I could do without. I had friends who offered to teach me to swim but I knew from past experience I was a loner when developing new skills. Besides, I anticipated a long haul and possible failure – if not drowning. Finally, I decided each morning right after Bill left for work I'd take an hour and hope I'd be the only swimmer at the hotel pool.

I started out slowly, just practicing floating, then I'd try getting across the pool without touching down. I had watched enough movies to know arm movement was important. Pretty soon I was able to go two widths. But I knew I had to swim a length. There was no way I'd jump in at the deep end, so I crawled down the ladder and crept along the edge to the deep end. If I had slipped it would have been the end of my illustrious swimming career but I got to the end, pushed myself off with my feet and actually got to the shallow end, water logged to be sure, but elated. I practiced for several days and could swim (to use the term loosely) six lengths before I told Bill;

"I've learned how to swim, honey!"

"Come on Bets, you'd drown in the bath tub."

"Alright smart ass, I'll have you a race! Five dollars to the winner."

The bet was on. I hadn't meant to race anyone but in the heat of the moment I had opened my big mouth. The great race was to be held Sunday – four days to practice. A young Canadian who was visiting the island saw me at the pool each morning. When I told him what I had got myself into he very gallantly helped me perfect my style which was a cross between an Australian crawl and a Dog Paddle. He told me not to worry!

When Sunday came I was very tempted to develop a serious problem like a sprained back. But no way, and I found myself at the pool at the appointed time. Allan was there and informed Bill he would be the judge and jumped in the pool. We were to race to the end of the pool and back. Being as how Bill was longer than me, Allan decided I should have a head start. It was a dead heat the first length but he was a good two feet ahead of me on the last lap. All of the sudden he faltered – as I hit the edge I glanced over and saw to my delight, Allan's foot placed firmly on Bill's shoulder.

By the time we left Niue I was anticipating taking Deep Sea Diving lessons – but that is now placed on the back burner.

Pom Poms and Celebrations

A unique and quite wonderful opportunity came my way after we were on Niue about a year. I had located the public library before we were even settled in our little house. It was quite small but had a good variety of books and I enjoyed browsing through them. I also got to know the head librarian, Ligi Sisakefu And. I would have a visit each time I returned books.

One very hot and humid day I was in the library, I had signed out my books but was not in any great rush to face the heat; so I just stood talking away in the coolness of the little dark room. Ligi seemed to be very interested in what I was doing, or wasn't doing, if I was bored etc. Finally she asked me "Betsy, we are planning an activity program to run through the school holidays in May. Can you help us?" It seemed a group of people would provide a bit of variety for the children in five of the villages during their school break. It would not only ensure a continuity of library interest and also provide another means of library service to the community in the villages.

I love something new and different so I jumped at the chance − even before I knew what was expected of me. The "group" turned out to be Ligi, her assistant, Reverend Paea, a Niuean minister who received his training in a Presbyterian College in New Zealand and I.

Reverend Paea was going to show a film on the neighbouring island of Takelau and lead some songs. Then we were to teach various activities: writing short stories and making a book, making book markers, making small containers out of old plastic bottles, creative drawings and the ladies of the village we were visiting were to teach the kids how to make grass skirts and toys out of native materials. Ligi was so enthusiastic! I asked just what I could help with. "Oh, just think of a fun craft for the kids to make, Betsy. I'm sure you will come up with something!" Little did she know me! I'm the least crafty person on earth! Even the aprons I used to make years ago for our church guild were a disaster – some I took apart three times – some I even buried. But I really wanted to be part of this excursion!

I said, "Sure", and went home wondering what in the devil I could make. I thought, and thought and finally in utter desperation decided I'd teach them how to make woollen pom poms.

I had two weeks to plan and prepare. First I had to get a huge sheet of fine cardboard, which took a bit of doing in itself. I finally located some at the little office of U.S.P. (University of the South Pacific).

Then I dug out all my own bits of yarn and begged and borrowed from all our neighbours. I cut circles out of the card board, not knowing how may children to plan for on the first day.

I was ready and waiting when Ligi phoned me, "Betsy, we have a problem. Have you any old bleach bottles or other plastic ones? I just can't find enough." I told her I'd look and ask Tui and Rosie if they had some. I finally collected about seven but she needed enough for kids in five villages! Then I remembered. When I was a kid I used to go to the town dump for treasures. There was something quite wonderful and exciting about town dumps. I never knew what I'd find, and many times I'd come home with weird things which I thought were the kings jewels, much to my mother's dismay. Why not try the Niuean dump! Of course, I was no kid now but what the heck – if anyone questioned me pawing through the dump I'd be able to say Ligi needed help. I climbed into my shorts and sneakers and ran over to get Tui. There was nothing too far out for Tui. She was game for anything my overactive mind devised.

So off we went with three empty garbage bags and a

"pocket full of dreams."

We found piles of empty bottles of all shapes and sizes but we couldn't stop there. No, our curiosity was great and my, what finds! A box full of childrens clothes patterns, an old hammer I was sure I could fix, a chunk of page wire for Tui's chicken coop, all things weird and wonderful.

We wiped our hands on the wet grass and headed out with our treasures. We stopped for a pop at K mart and went home delighted. Of course, I then had to wash off all the bottles – a big job. One by one at first, then I got weary and decided to put about six at a time into my washer, and let it have a go at it. The next day I gave three bags full to Ligi.

Our first program was to be tested out at Hacupu Village on May 16. We all travelled in a big van, four of us along with all our paraphernalia, craft materials, projector, pots to cook the lunch we were going to serve and the rice and paw paws. Our spirits were soaring as we bumped along, Ligi driving. It was held in the schoolroom, which was full of kids by the time we arrived.

All went smoothly at first. The songs Rev. Paea lead were sung gustily, as only little kids can. When I was introduced there was much excitement, "She's the lady with the Magic Mirror!" Soon we settled down with our projects. Some village Mamas helped and all went well until the first pom poms were made and passed around. This was something new and different. Many had never seen one, never mind seen one made. In a matter of seconds every kid was leaping around me begging to make pom poms. It was utter chaos! I had only four or five big balls of wool and one pair of scissors. I'd roll off enough yarn for one kid, start them on the cardboard circles and by then the wool would be across the room. The scissors would be in a pocket somewhere, I cannot describe the bedlam. In desperation Ligi came to my rescue, even Rev. Paea had to be recruited into dishing out wool, cutting and tying.

Lunch was served at 1:00 p.m. We had cooked a huge pot of rice, cut paw paws in strips and had chunks of coconut all eaten off (lau le) big shiny leaves.

On the way home we discussed the mornings events. I decided to maintain any semblance of order I'd have to get busy and roll enough yarn to make one pom pom into individual balls, quite a chore as there had been thirty-one kids at Hacupu and we expected more at Avatele, the next village we were to visit in two days.

Ligi was pleased. There had been great interest shown. When we arrived at Avatele there were fifty-three kids, and lots of moms and grandmas and a great time was had by all, but the pom pom-making was a war zone once more, only now the moms and grandmas were also making them and the kids three or more each. The scissors would be gone, the yarn rolling around the floor, and one old lady had her new pom pom tied about her waist and was dancing a whirling derwish up the middle of the room.

So we finally decided, to save my sanity, I'd have to ration them to one pom pom each and Ligi thought they should make one other item first. This was wise as in Avalele there had been sixty-six pom poms and only little numbers of our other projects.

The two weeks went by so quickly. We still had a bedlam at the pom pom corner but we could handle it now without too big a fuss.

The program attracted a good number of people, interest and participation was high. It was quite hilarious. Bruce, a high school teacher, told me he had seen pom poms at school on both boys and girls and everywhere I went for weeks after I'd see pom poms decorating everything from a dog's neck to the dusty picture of Queen Elizabeth tacked on the wall.

There are many unique colourful ceremonies within the lifestyle of the Niuean people, the haircutting ceremony is one of these.

At one time this ceremony took place when a boy reached puberty but now, more realistically, it is held when the family has the means and the time to hold it. It is now a spiritual as well as moneymaking scheme, at times raising as much as $30,000 for a first male child. Of course it takes months of preparation on the part of the family. There are pigs to raise, as many as possible, taro, hundreds of plants to plant and weed, fish to catch. If freezers facilities are available the men would start months ahead. Right up until the great event the women will be baking, hunting for land crabs and the men will be hunting for flying foxes and pigeons. Hundreds of people are invited and as well as giving gifts, they are also expected to give money. The taro, corned beef, fish, pork, indeed all the food the family has collected will be given to the guests – the portions are decided by the amount of the money gift.

A young boy's haircut –
an old traditional celebration.

Huge shelters made of palm branches are erected which the guests sit under. The honoured boy sits on a chair which is covered by lengths of cloth. His hair, which can be very long, is parted and tied in many little tufts, each tied with ribbon. The guests spend the whole day, although the actual ceremony doesn't take that long. Several family members and honoured guests each cut one tuft of hair, some just cutting, but others giving long speeches or prayers. I attended one and it was especially moved when an old grandmother shyly stepped forth and cut her piece on her beloved grandson's special day.

The Umus are opened and the food served.

While the ceremony is taking place, relatives place the butchered pigs on huge leaves and are chopping them apart into small pieces, with knives and even axes and the food is then laid out on the ground in piles. One row for $500 gifts, one for $200 and so on down to the $40 or $50 gifts. A gift of $500 would bring half a pig or at least a quarter, lots of fish, a pigeon, crab, taro and other food like a big can of corned beef. Of course, the $50 size would only get a little pork, a taro and maybe a fish or two.

The master of ceremonies will call out the names of the guests and all will step forth and collect their food gift. There is much merriment and dancing the whole day. The girls' equivalent of the haircutting is the earpiercing ceremony. This is basically the same, except the girl gets more gifts and it's a favoured aunt or some other special person who actually pierces the ear.

Traditionally, it is done with a sharp long thorn but now sterilized needles are sometimes used and some of the girls even have a doctor freeze their earlobes before the actual ceremony. I attended one earpiercing which collected enough money to buy a good used car and a huge coloured television.

I know to western ears this sounds dreadfully mercenary but it is not unlike our celebrations. The families work very hard and spend a considerable amount of money and the guests get their moneys worth. Indeed at our weddings the gifts the guests bring are very expensive and all we get out of it (besides the joy of giving) is a wedding lunch and a Thank you card! These people go home with a gift of food. A letter from a Niuean friend gave this as a list of the food they had raised and bought for her daughter's earpiercing: Taro, nine thousand; Fish, forty-eight; Beef and Pork carcasses sixty-three; Kegged Beef, forty; Chickens, twenty; six-pound cans of Corned Beef, thirteen; three pound cans of Corned Beef, six. They made a total of $31,000 that day!

I might add, the customs at weddings, birthdays or any holiday celebration there is an immense pile of food of all types piled on tables. Each Mama brings an empty basket which she rushes to fill from the ladened tables. This food is taken home rather than eaten at the celebration. I often wondered about this custom as the taro would be left whole, the cans of Corned Beef would be unopened and none of the food was in serving dishes. If it was a huge affair where many Polagis were invited the hosts would set a separate table English style and invite the whites to come forth and sit but the rest all went into the baskets. I attended a few of these and always felt strange, but after I saw even Lady Rex filling her basket I felt it was fine for me to do also.

The Niuean people are predominately Protestants and their church and their Sunday is very important to them. In nearly every village is at least one church and each Sunday you'll see the families going.

The white population could attend either the Catholic church or the little Protestant one started by Reverend Alf Paea who felt the white protestants needed an English speaking service. Alf was a very dedicated and fine human being and he and his wife, Margaret, laboured long and hard for this little church. Alf, a Niuean, was a trainee in a Presbyterian College in New Zealand and had his own parish in New Zealand for years.

The building the services were held in was a battered one near the reef. It wasn't much to look at but on Sunday morning it took on new life, despite the small congregation.

A congregation of ten or twelve on Sunday morning was average. But Alf was an optimist. There was no piano or organ but a Niuean lady led the singing gustily, strumming like mad on her guitar. It went very well. Of course there was some friction among the congregation but with most postings being a two year stint, most differences disappeared as one or more of the antagonists would move on in due time.

Alf had a wonderful Sunday School in many villages and the children loved him. He was well respected by all and with his hearty laugh and sense of humour he was welcome in any home he visited. Margaret, a jolly lady, often accompanied me on my village run. One interesting point occurred the day of communion was served; Alf used coconut milk as communion wine – a very nice choice I felt.

Christmas is a big celebration on Niue, a real family time. Our first was on us so quickly and I had little time to prepare. We were invited to a regular Niuean Christmas dinner at Fine's. Fine was the school librarian, a wonderfully jolly lady. They had decorated the house with coloured paper links and had a twig tree decorated. But it was strange to sing Christmas hymns with flowers in bloom and the temperature at 29° C.

Typical Niuean dressed for a celebration.

The next Christmas, however, we were acclimatized and had prepared ahead.

The farm had a row of Norfolk Pines so Bill chopped off a good big branch and stuck it in a bucket of stones. I had brought a few unbreakable ornaments with me and I made a few out of silver paper. Most of the parcels from home arrived on time and so spirits were high.

Annette and Paul invited us for Xmas breakfast at 8:00 a.m. but at 6:00 a.m. little Jon Jon was over tapping on the door, "Betty, Bill, come and watch us open our gifts, Dad's going to video it." all in his strong Kiwi accent. So up we got. It felt strange putting on my makeup at 6:00 a.m. – eye shadow and all. Even on Christmas Day Paul wasn't going to catch me on video without makeup – besides I doubt his camera could handle it! After a special breakfast we went home and dressed for a 10:00 a.m. cocktail party at another neighbours place which was a mite different than what we were used to.

At supper we were all invited down to Mirium's. Mirium was a Niuean lady who ran the sewing factory, Barry, Bill and I were the only whites there but by then we felt quite Niuean! Another very special holiday for all Niueans is the old custom of celebrating the birth of Christ and welcoming for the New Year. This is held the first Saturday of January when they decorate cars, trucks and motorbikes and ride around the whole island visiting at each village with much singing and good cheer. The Niuean name for this holiday is "Takai."

The Niuean ladies near Alofi formed a group to play "Housie," which is a form of Bingo. There were about forty members when I joined. It was held once a month and everyone took turns hosting it. I'm not a big Bingo fan but this was different. It allowed me to visit amongst the the Niueans which I really loved. We didn't play for a lot of money but what there was we all fought to win.

Tui and I rarely missed a game and I managed to host it once before we returned home. Knowing full well that the lunch I prepared would have to be large enough to serve that night as well as leave some for the members to take home, I baked up a fury. My one and only worry was the size of my house but we shoved everything back and all sat on the floor. By this time I was completely at home with the ladies and they had accepted me so a snorting great time was had.

Medical Mania

Niue is free from many tropical diseases such as Malaria and Cholera, with very few outbreaks of any disease. But every once in awhile there is an epidemic of "Dengue Fever". A tropical fever caused by mosquito bites. But a person must be very careful of infection, even a very little scratch can become infected very quickly.

Niue however, has a good hospital. Sparse to some eyes, but certainly good for a developing country. The staff was all Niuean with some assistance from visiting specialists from New Zealand from time to time and senior student doctors are there on a regular basis, taking their Tropical Apprenticeship. General medicine, surgery, obstetrics and outpatient services are all provided free-of-charge.

In serious or extra-complicated cases patients can be sent to New Zealand for treatment. There were two or three emergencies while we were there, one man was in grave danger of losing an eye after a gun accident, so was immediately airlifted to New Zealand, but the staff on Niue could handle many other accidents.

Dr. Harry Nemaia was the "hub" of the hospital, an extremely fine human being and a very caring physician. Dr. Harry was a clever man, he told me he had been a dentist but tired of it and thought the field of medicine more challenging.

The nurses were all islanders who trained either in Fiji or New Zealand. The hospital like all tropical ones is open and airy – cement floors and louvered windows. There are the ghecos crawling the walls and ceilings but it was clean as could be.

It was different in some ways however. The meals were very sparse. There just wasn't enough money to provide anything but small very basic meals – A bit of rice and meat, usually corned beef in a thin sauce or mutton sausages. But most all patients had food brought in by their families.

When a patient arrived they would be accompanied by two, three or even four of their kith and kin, pillows all decked out in the finest embroidered cases and mats. The mats were for the relatives to sleep on as they stayed day and night sometimes for the duration of the patients' stay in hospital. I witnessed this first hand.

While rushing about one day I slipped on a wet spot on my cement floor and went crashing down. I got through the day okay, hoping it is just a sprain, but next morning I was in so much pain I caught a ride to the hospital where I had my ankle x-rayed. Sure enough – broken.

Dr. Nemaia put me in the hospital until the swelling went down he said he would then cast it. It proved to be quite an adventure. My roommate was a Niuean girl who had had a motorbike accident and I really enjoyed her as she was boistrous and happy, shouting to friends out in the street and giggling with the nurses. Both of us needed a wheelchair to go anywhere and the bathroom was quite a distance which we had to wheel along the outside sidewalk to reach. I have trouble with a wheelbarrow never mind a wheelchair so I was always ramming into walls and posts much to the amusement of the staff. At night her relatives would bed down on the floor and were truly mystified when Bill wouldn't bring his mat and sleep at the foot of my bed. I never lacked for company, however. Being the only Polagi in the hospital I was a bit of a curiosity piece and all guests would troop through to gaze at me – some in wonderment, some in merriment.

Several nights if it was extra cold or was storming the nurses going off duty would find a mat or a piece of foam and come and sleep beside my bed rather than driving home to their villages. Of course they'd try out all my make-up and perfume first. It was a common sight to see three or four nurses perched on every corner of my bed chattering away while applying nail polish and lipstick and good shots of cologne. They took turns combing my hair and painting my toenails along with theirs. I didn't mind. I certainly wasn't sick and they were making dead sure I wasn't bored.

I truly believe however, that our sterile quiet institutions in the Western world with their visiting restrictions should take a look at the Niueans. Patients need the comfort and closeness of loved ones, their own pillows and food, although I also realize this unique practice would throw a very large monkey wrench into the working gears of a huge city hospital. Dr. Harry kept me flat out for sometime before he casted my ankle. Then he gave me a walking cast. It was quite inventive. He took the sole of an old thong, folded it in half crossways, and tied it on the bottom of my cast. On questioning him he told me with the ever present financial problems he always looked for ways to economize. The funny thing was it worked much better, and was easier to walk on then the real ones! It worked so well I walked so much the first day I had it I cracked the cast and had to go for a patch job.

One day Godfrey, our Sri Lankan friend, was driving his motorbike hell for leather over a country road and took quite a tumble. He broke his collar bone and was scratched on more skin surface than you can imagine. (What the natives call "gravel rash.") Anyway, he was in real pain with the collarbone and Rosie spent all her time with him. Tui and I took turns with the boys, but Rosie's place was with Godfrey. She'd cook his own special meals at home and bring them in, and sit with him, fanning him with a little woven fan all day and most of each night. Godfrey was okay but Rosie was coming apart from lack of sleep and worry.

The doctors tried to tell her all this loving attention wasn't necessary but Rosie was adamant. Tui and I tried to bring her home to sleep but she replied, "No, my place is beside Godfrey!" While I admired her devotion I felt we'd have two sick friends instead of one! I had dreams of her throwing herself on a funeral pyre, as in olden days in Sri Lanka!

As for medical assistance for the villages, each had a red flag and a team of a doctor and one or two nurses would visit two or three times a week. They'd drive through all the villages stopping wherever they saw the red flag raised knowing there was a patient there.

Dental care was also free. There were two dentists, one lived in our settlement and was so handsome you would gasp. The first time I saw him he was practicing his golfing on the green and had inadvertently hit the ball into our flower bed. I heard a rustling out front so went to see what was up, thinking the wild chickens must be scratching about. I opened the door in time to see him lift his big straw hat and bow low. "Good morning madam," he said gallantly as he wiped his golf ball and strode off.

Young doctors from New Zealand would come for three or four months for tropical medicine training and we met many of them. They usually mixed with one and all and we hated to see them go. One female doctor eventually married Tony, a friend who was a FAO field corp specialist, after she met him while on Niue.

Another female doctor met a young Tongan mechanic and they fell in love. She went back to New Zealand after her term and he followed. I never did hear how that great love affair ended.

The Farm

While I was gadding about "my island" Bill, who made it all possible, was trying, sometimes in vain, to make a viable working cattle operation out of the farm. A monumental task to say the least.

The total farm area amounted to 1,211 acres – 274 of these at the Vaiea farm where the headquarters were. The rest was spread over several blocks close to the villages of Haiupa, Liku, Lakepa, and Mutalau.

When Bill arrived the whole area was completely overgrown with blue snake weed or "blue rats' tail" as the Niueans called it. It was a dreadful mess, caused by poor farm management and overgrazing and thus the cattle eating out all the grass and legume. In order to clean these weeds out the Niuean Development Board (NDB) agreed on a crash program of weed eradication and applied for a grant from the Australian government amounting to $80,000 for the restoration of Vaiea farm. It was a formidable task – 274 acres had to be either hand weeded or slashed with a bush knife. One hundred acres needed complete clearing and resowing. It was hoped the remaining acres once cleared would re-establish themselves.

There were somewhere between 300 to 400 head of cattle, pasturing under the coconut trees. The cattle grazing kept the grass down so coconuts could be found. Bill's first immense problem was feed. With the severe drought the cattle were starving. With the farm divided into paddocks the idea was to rotate by number but with the drought and very poor fences it was hopeless. The cattle wandered over the whole island.

The first thing Bill did was order 100 or so head butchered for local use. In order to feed the remaining 200 he took the big lorry and six of his best workers and drove all over the island in search of patches of elephant grass which they cut and tossed in the truck. This for 200 cows?! It was like spitting in a cloud to make rain, it even became so desperate they chopped coconuts and fed it to the cows but this too was a lesson in futility as coconut had to be dug out of the shells by hand!

The big farm truck was used every day –
all vehicles are very rusty, as can be seen in the picture.

He also tried feeding the fruit skins from the lime and passion fruit which he collected from the food processing factory. He also organized a crew to cut branches of trees to feed.

With a lot of persuasion and red tape they finally had a boat load of feed shipped in from New Zealand which was a big relief. When he arrived he noticed great sacks of grass seed in a shed for replanting, but when planted it wouldn't germinate. Some foreign company had sluffed it off on the Niueans.

Bill's crew of workers consisted of six girls and eight men. The girls were good workers, all in their teens with one girl,

Lower Hutt, as the self proclaimed foreman. She was an energetic and hard worker who wouldn't allow others to shirk their duty as she saw it. Bill felt he could get twice as much work out of the crew if Lower Hutt was there. So he managed to get her a raise to show his appreciation and also to possibly give the others incentive to try harder.

Lower Hutt, although very forward with the workers, felt ill-at-ease with me. Bill often stopped by our house for cold juice if he had his crew in town and the first time this happened Lower Hutt wouldn't come in, instead she took the flower off my lipstick plant and painted tribal designs on her face and when I approached her with my tray of juice she, in false bravado, snorted, "I want a beer!!" But she soon felt comfortable with me and we became good friends.

Lisa was another of my favourites. Her parents were in New Zealand and she lived with her Grandmother and Grandfather at Vaiea Village. They were the real epitome of Niuean natives, gentle, kindly, proud people.

Bill's hands were full enough with the drought and starving cattle but he also encountered another very big and complex problem before we were even in our home. This was cattle rustling. "The powers that be," in Central Office blamed it on the shortage of feed which caused the cattle to jump the fences for fresh grazing. This practice was widespread and took place when the cattle strayed away as well in the paddocks, and had been going on for some time. It's not too difficult to understand the indignation of Niueans who found the cows in their damaged gardens. I know how I feel if our cattle get into my garden in Alberta but I, despite the urge, never shot them. Still it was a well-known and accepted fact that unjustified rustling was taking place. This "meat on the hoof" was a wonderful and acceptable extra for special ceremonies like haircutting or earpiercing.

When Bill arrived there were fourteen bulls, but in two months he was down to four and of course these were the scrawniest ones! The rustlers always picked the best. During December and January there are many Fia Fias and B.B.Q.s.

"It's the silly season," Bill was told, "They will quit soon." The Niueans felt the cattle were theirs, not the UN's or the government's, they belonged to the people.

Of course Bill was irate to say the least. "Back home we used to hang men for rustling!"

He took the problem to the Police as well as the government but to no avail. The Police were involved as were government officials, which is really no different than our own country. It's just in our country the graft and corruption is hidden in anonymity of the large area.

When Bradley Puno and his wife Lisa moved back to Niue and Bradley became Minister of Agriculture, he decided that being as so many visitors called at the experimental station they should take two healthy calves from the farm there for show purposes. Bill did and would you believe by the next morning they were rustled, nary hide nor hair could be found!

The traditional Niuean lifestyle was one of sharing everything. Mother Earth provided the food stuffs and all owned it. So I can understand the rustling when seen through a native's eyes.

But Bill couldn't afford to lose anymore. He had the cattle moved to the farm headquarters and proceeded to build a fence so high and strong an elephant would be held in.

Getting the fence erected was quite a chore in itself. The posts are all concrete so they wouldn't rot. The wires were smooth because barbed wire would rust due to the climate and humidity. Dropper posts were placed at regular intervals and two more strands put on top. The men tried to get out of fencing, it was hard work, especially when a depth of soil of six inches is good and below that is solid rock. The cattle at least were contained, but there were still losses. One particular time Bill found out about a loss and went out to the paddock, camera in hand. He found the spot where the cow had been butchered and dug up the remains, also finding an empty shot gun shell. He took pictures for proof but nothing came of it.

To illustrate the thinking of Niueans, Bill and I were at a

great celebration at the Parliament building one evening and a Niuean came up to Bill,

"Bill, I helped you today!"

"Oh really, in what way?"

"I know a man who was going to shoot a cow, he was going to cut the fence to get it but I told him, "No, Bill worked hard on that fence, you shoot it in the paddock and lift the meat over." "

On investigation by the UNDP it was figured within a two year period over 200 animals graced the rustling stewpot. I tasted some of this illicit meat. On our tour of villages with the librarian we were sitting down to eat our rice when a village lady brought over a pot full of meat and greens, "Betsy, you must eat our Niuean Beef!"

I did – it was delicious!

Bill's Foreman was a lovable rascal, Sefo Lui. The first time I met Sefo I immediately thought of a rough copy of Charlie Chan. The moustache, the eyes, everything. He was married to a pretty gentle lady Olive, (pronounced Oliv ee.) They had a large family, eight kids, and were poor in comparison to some in the village but seemed happy together. Olive was pregnant when we arrived and when a big baby girl was born they did me a great honor by naming her "Betsy"; I'm known as Betty to most everyone but Bill, and his nickname for me is "Betsy." Of course, that's all Olive and Sefo heard me called so the baby was, and is, "Betsy".

Betsy and her namesake.

Sefo should be in politics as he played the system every moment of every day. In fact everytime Bill came home from work he'd have another "Sefo story." By the end of our tour of duty all the neighbours were greeting him with: "What did Sefo try today?!"

In addition to being Foreman, Sefo was also the butcher. The farm butchered at least once a week. The abbatoir was situated near our settlement, and adjacent to this building were paddocks to contain the cattle. In 1981 a senior veterinarian officer from Australia visited the abbatoir privately. His findings were a bit alarming. In his view there was a real risk of Salmonella poisoning breaking out. The Director of Health closed it until it had been extensively renovated. But when I saw the building it was sanitary and well-kept. A woman was hired to weigh and wrap the meat destined for private homes and local stores.

Bill's crew – Sefo lying in front.

Sefo, being such a good butcher, was also hired by locals, Polagi and Niuean, to butcher their pigs. This was "after hours" work and he would be paid money or pork. One of the stories I heard follows. He was called in to butcher a pig for a Polagi, but when the meat was returned there were only three legs! The fellow went to Sefo and informed him, "That pig had four legs when I brought it in – now there is only three!" But Sefo, ever a step ahead stated, "I am the Meat Inspector and that one leg was condemned by me!"

The man wasn't backing down. "I want to see it – this condemned leg!"

"Oh, I had to throw it away before it contaminated the other meat!"

"Take me to where you threw it then."

So off they went, finally coming to a cave which could only be reached by climbing down a rope. "It's down there," stated Sefo.

A rope was retrieved and the man expected Sefo to climb down but no – Sefo grinned, "No I can't go down there – *Aitu* (spirits)." The man looked at the rope, then Sefo and knew he was beat. If he went down the rope Sefo could very easily let the rope drop and the poor fellow would be there without a means of getting out again. Sefo won another round!

Just once did Bill get the best of Sefo. Bill and Okati had gone to town. Okati bought two dozen bottles of beer, took them back to the farm and handed them out to the men; all but Sefo. My he was disgusted! Soon they were all roaring drunk, all except Sefo. Bill turned to Sefo and stated, "Sefo, we have got to stop this drinking at work."

So they called a meeting to inform all the workers that anyone caught drinking at work would be terminated. Sefo feeling so self-righteous forgot for the moment that when the opportunity arose he was the worst offender.

Bill's days were full but he soon had things under control. One thing he really felt would help the cattle herd was a good breeding program using Polled Hereford bulls. He took this suggestion to the Director of Agriculture, Bradley Puno, who agreed with it. He told Bill to check into the feasibility of locating two good yearlings in New Zealand. We were planning on spending our month holiday in New Zealand with Bill attending the world Hereford conference in Christchurch and this he did. He located some at Ken Williams, a breeder near Aukland. On returning to the island enough paper work was carried out to paper the Parliament Buildings and the end result was two yearling Polled Herefords finally arriving on Niue a few months after we returned to Alberta. The last word was, they were fine, healthy and as yet, not rustled.

At various times during Bill's tenure as Farm Manager he was blessed either positively or negatively depending on who came, with visits from the UN office in Samoa and other islands. Some were really fine people and our favourite of these visitors was Dr.Hussain, a Pakistani who was the FAO Animal Production Officer posted to Tonga. He and Bill got along famously and could discuss all types of programs which would benefit the farm. He was above all, a gentleman of the old school.

Another visitor was an English veterinarian stationed on Fiji. He spent a great deal of time informing us colonists how he was proud to be an Englishman but in the midst of this vocalizing is an interesting story. I had asked him if he had met James Herriot the famous veterinarian who wrote of his own experiences in such a delightful way. "Yes, I at one time had a country practice that bordered that of James Herriot." But he said he was sure all veterinarians have similar weird experiences if they just had the talent to put it down on paper.

As an illustration he told me this tale. There were two old maid missionary sisters retired within his area. They were gentle, kind and only slightly mad, possibly eccentric. For one thing they dearly loved animals which wasn't odd but their choice of pets was. Their favourite was a tame seven foot alligator which they kept in the backyard in good weather and in a run in the basement when the weather was chilly. One good point was the old dears never had to worry about prowlers but the bad point was they had to buy chickens by the dozen to feed "Big A."

Gradually the poor creature ate less and less and "lost

some of his bounce" as the ladies put it. Dr. Seville had treated many and varied animals but alligators he knew little about. He tried in vain to find any material on alligator ailments with little success. Finally, he asked the ladies if "Big A" was constipated. "Why yes, his poo (said with a blush) is little, far between and terribly smelly! It was off colour as well."

He didn't know just what "off colour" meant concerning alligator excrement but he took them at their word. So what to do with a constipated alligator. Mineral Oil, But how! So chickens were liberally soaked in mineral oil but he wouldn't eat them. It ended up the vet, a man for all seasons, sat on the creatures back and pried its jaws apart. The two old ladies tossed in the chickens loaded with mineral oil, as each chicken was tossed in the vet would let loose and let it swallow it. Soon all the chickens were gone and the tired vet went home to bed.

Next morning he checked the creature, thinking it should have loosened up and be feeling better, but still no results. They dipped some more chickens in oil and as the vet stepped over the creature to pry its jaws open he stumbled and landed with all his weight on the creatures back. Lo and behold out popped a huge egg! "Big A" was a female. The vet read later that alligators, can and do, become egg bound. This condition can even cause death. So "Big A" was cured and in fine form except as the old dears said, "His poo was dreadfully loose" for a few days.

One time two fellows from FAO, a Finn and an American, arrived to see Bill and his farm. After their business was conducted they had time to do a bit of sightseeing. They wondered if Bill could show them the ocean from the west side of the island as they had never been there. Bill is very fit and able but he wondered about these two from behind desks, they looked a mite soft but off they went. It was a real hike; rough, through thick raw forest over rocks of all sizes. The American had the hardest time as he was wearing shiny black patent shoes and slid with every step. However, he also sported a toupee which caught in the branches. And he would have to stop and collect it, to jam back on his shiny dome once more.

They visited a cave situated in the middle of the island but was entered by climbing down a rope, reversing this procedure to get back out. They decided they weren't too interested in climbing down – especially when Bill pointed out the skulls and other bones looking too human to please the men. It was an old burial cave and no Niuean would go down into it nor would these gentlemen. They visited the abattoir also but the Finn felt he might be sick if they checked the killing floor. All in all I believe they were glad to be back to the civilization of Samoa.

New Zealand Bound

We were on Niue for fifteen months when we finalized our plans. we were to fly to New Zealand, for a month holiday, visiting friends and attending the World Hereford Conference which was being held in Christchurch on the South Island.

Several years before, back at home in Alberta, we used to be a part of the International Agriculture Exchange Program, having had several boys from Sweden, Denmark and New Zealand. Rex Davis was one of these. He was a real addition to the Kilgour clan and was loved by all. Of course, when the season was over he went back to New Zealand, bought a farm and married the girl who waited for him and they now have four children. We had kept in touch with him through the years and his mother and sister had visited us in Alberta while on a world tour so we really looked forward to seeing them all once more.

Our next door neighbours on Niue, Paul and Annette Galland and their two small children, had finished their posting and were back home in Wellington by this time. Although they had been gone but a few weeks I missed them dreadfully. I spent a great deal of time with Annette, and Jon and Nikki were like my own, in fact our house was just an extended room for Jon.

We flew out planning on stopping in Auckland to get some dry cleaning done and run some errands. Then Bill would go to the Conference and I'd continue on to Rex's mother's home in Oamaru. But when we landed in Aukland lo and behold there was Rex, his wife Brenda and his whole family. He had taken the kids out of school and had driven 200 miles into Aukland.

He hadn't changed a bit! The rest of the holiday went by very quickly.

I stayed with Harri, Rex's mother, and shopped like I been locked away for years. I tended to buy strange things – spices, walnuts, hair perms everything I couldn't get on Niue. We also ripped up old sheets for diapers, unraveled sweaters for yarn and bought some yarn at the woollen mill. I collected old knitting needles from all Harri's friends and some old clothes which I shipped in six huge boxes home to Niue. Still my suitcases were absolutely bulging!

The Post Office was a tad different. They had a lax way of running it. When I shipped the six big boxes off from New Zealand I had fun. When the mail was sorted I went in, "We haven't checked all the boxes yet Betty, but come and look." I did but only found three of them. I told him they were all shipped the same time and there should be more. "Don't worry Betty, they will show up."

I checked through customs, "What's in there," I was asked.

"Old clothes, knitting needles, torn sheets."

"What is all that for?"

"Oh, just for the Vaiea ladies and the new babies."

"Oh well, for the Niueans – no charge."

When I got home, there lo and behold were the remaining boxes on my doorsteps.

And we want to turn these beautiful laid back people into a bunch of little Englishman? No way – I love them the way they are.

Harri and I joined Bill for the last two days of the Hereford tour and enjoyed the scenery. I don't think I've ever seen such a variety of scenery, all majestic, all beautiful. The life style of the New Zealanders was more peaceful, "they take time to smell the roses." Bill and I both felt if we didn't have a home country we could settle into the New Zealand lifestyle very easily.

As we worked our way back we spent three days with the Gatlands. It was nice to see them in their little home but it was harder than ever to say good bye, even though the world is such a small place, Canada is a long way off.

Our month was up before we knew it and we flew out from Aukland landing in Apia some three hours later. We managed to get a room in the same little hotel we had been registered in when we started out on our island adventure fifteen months previous. But now we felt we were seasoned travellers! I went to sleep feeling contented knowing I'd be back on Niue the next afternoon, we had missed the place!

But this wasn't to be. We boarded the plane and took off, but once we were over the ocean I thought something is strange.

"Bill, isn't this plane going awfully slow?!"

"Maybe. It's not gaining altitude either."

He glanced out the window and noticed the leading edge flaps, which are extended on take-off, wouldn't slide back in. One caught on the edge and the one on the opposite wing twisted off. The plane was shuddering like it had massive hicc-ups.

The pilot slowly banked the plane around and came over the speaker, "We have a slight problem, fasten all safety belts and no smoking. We are returning to Apia and will be landing at a slightly faster speed than usual."

The passengers started crying and screaming and nothing had happened yet! We came in very low over the water and I kept thinking, "I'm sure glad I learned how to swim – in case we ditch!" We touched down with a good few bumps and the "slightly faster speed than usual" was the understatement of the day – the force put such a strain on the safety belts I had bruises for weeks. The first thing I noticed were the three firetrucks we passed in a blur. The pilot got the plane stopped at the end of the runway and everyone clapped like mad.

One fellow hopped out to take pictures but the police nabbed him. They didn't want pictures of the heaps of rubber we had left as we seared along the length of the runway. We were all herded into the airport and we stood about, still sha- key. The first man I noticed was the squeamish Finn who turned green when Bill showed him the bones in the burial cave. He told us he always been scared of flying, and he was deathly white.

But a wonderful thing happened, after they checked over the plane and served us sandwiches we were all taken by bus to stay the night at Aggie Greys Hotel, no less. As I've told you, Aggie Greys is the "Hilton deluxe" of the islands. My it was delightful. I lapped up the luxury like a dry sponge. We were all invited to a great island feast and song that night, with the island dancers, flame dancers, the whole bit! We stayed for two nights and got to go on a guided tour of Samoan villages and scenic sites during the day. I was gloating about our stroke of luck so much Bill told Bob that he was sure I had prayed for this to happen, it was the only way I'd ever get to stay at Aggie Greys. I probably would have too, if I'd thought of it!

But what a thrill to be circling over Niue once more. As we come in and taxied back we could pick out all our friends there to greet us. What a homecoming and we had been gone only a month. About twenty little kids packed against the fence as we walked by and I stopped to talk to them. One little boy went home and told his mother "Mommy, can you believe Betsy still knows my name!" One month is a long time for a child.

Leaving Niue

In July 1984 we knew our term would be up the end of September but we could hardly believe two years, minus a month, would soon be over.

The dining room set Bob Pope made for us was ready and the crate to carry it made so we decided to pack as much as we could into all the available space between chair legs etc. I dragged out all the sheets and pillows, cushions and clothing I could. The many baskets and mats we had bought and received, and in general everything we could do without. I phoned Henry, our friend at Public Works and asked if we could use a survival kit. It was no problem he assured me, so I packed everything that the kit contained. It was off on the July boat and we hoped it would arrive in Canada by October. We also sent our trunk with the overflow. It's amazing what two people can collect in two years time.

Before we knew it September 1st had arrived as did our farewells. It was to be one of the most bittersweet months of our lives. I kept the September leaf off our calendar as I knew no one back home would believe me. We had only eight free days in September and some of the days had two or three events in them. Many of these were quiet suppers with friends but many were real tear-jerking galas!

The farm had a farewell B.B.Q. for Bill and I, with Barry and Tui invited. It was in the afternoon and Bill bought the beer. After much eating and drinking the speeches started. I think everyone spoke, and tried to outdo the other. Ender, a boy about sixteen, was the best. He ended by saying, "Do not worry Bill about these cows, when you are far away – we will

all take care of them." and he fell over his chair in his exuber-
ance, to thunderous applause.

The "housie" ladies had an evening for us at Kars
residence which was touching. They were doing impromptu
dances and much singing and merriment ending with a
presentation of a white ruffled bed throw with the Niue emblem
silk screened on it. They told me I had never won many games
but I had won their love. That was enough for for me!

But one real tearful one was the one the settlement
(Fualahi) staged. Leigh and Bob Sutton arranged it and all our
friends were there. It was one of those beautiful tropical nights
with perfume wafting about. By this time Tui and I were blue
and thinking of the parting ahead. Songs were sung so plain-
tively it nearly caused my demise. By the time it was over we
were all weeping. Even today four years later, I break out in
tears when I play the tape she gave me. I looked around at all
my friends and realized how far away I'd be. It was just two
years ago I felt this same ache when I left my children in
Alberta!

But the most moving farewell was the one arranged by the
ladies of Vaiea village. Bill had heard rumours and rustlings of
this event for weeks but he kept it secret. The ladies had taken
turns going out trapping coconut crabs, weaving gifts and making costumes. The men told Bill it was the first time they ever
staged one for a Polagi. In fact only people leaving their village
were so honoured.

Word was sent via by Bill of the evening we were to come.
When we arrived we were led to one house to wait while the
food was set out and it was just dark when we were escorted
back to the little hall where we had spent so many days
together, crocheting, making jam and pom poms. The table
was sagging under the weight of all the food. They knew I
loved crab and boy they had crab.

After the feast the women donned grass skirts and
flowers, even little four-year-olds, and they danced and sang in
Niuean, giving us leis as they sang. I was dragged up to
dance and so was Bill much to his embarrassment but he's a
good guy and went along.

My friends dance at our farewell.

Then Alf turned to me and said, "Betty they are going to sing special songs for you now," and he translated as they sang.

> Betty, you are leaving this little island and all of your friends here. But we won't forget you even if you forget us. But you can never leave Vaiea, now you are a member of our families and we are yours. No matter where you go you will take something of Vaiea with you. And as for us, we will never forget you!
> You are our mother, our sister, our aunty – we shall await your return!

I felt very humble, sitting there, as they came with kisses and gifts, I felt I was an imposter and didn't deserve this honour. These beautiful, gentle people with such dignity and love in their hearts. It was an evening I'll cherish forever.

There were other farewells and by the time the day arrived to fly out I was so tired I was almost a zombie. But the hardest parting was still ahead of me, to say goodbye to Tui and Barry.

We kept putting it off until we got to the airport. I was worried because stress was one thing Tui did not need. The airport was full of well-wishers and we had ten or more leis around and our necks, and our hands full of other gifts. Finally, as I was saying goodbye to Leigh (She being such a compassionate lady I knew she would understand completely) when I said "Please take care of Tui."

Tui and I just broke down but somehow Bill got me through the door.

Bill and I were wearing matching straw hats as we left. (Lisa's Grandma had made them for us.) As I approached on the steps to the plane the wind caught mine and sent it rolling down the runway; would you believe the pilot went to pick it up!

"Where else but on Niue!", I thought.

We arrived home safe and sound but it took me two weeks to get my days and nights straightened out. Our crates arrived Christmas Eve, just in time for a great family Christmas with all the new grandchildren.

The Niuean "Toi Wood" dining set is big enough for the whole clan to sit around and is our pride and joy. But what is more precious by far are our memories which I never need to polish.

Barry and Tui have since retired to live on Tui's land on Rarotonga, and spend part of each year in New Zealand where their daughter, Alice, lives with her husband and children. We had the good fortune of having Barry and Tui visit us for two months the summer of 1986. It was marvelous although I think Tui was chilly a great deal of the time.

Bruce and Eileen are back in Wellington and they have a new baby girl. Leigh and Bob are also back in New Zealand and have a daughter. It must have been the Niuean air! Annette and Paul, Jon and Nikki are in close contact as Jon and my grandson, Nathan, are pen pals. And Nikki is pen pals with my granddaughter, Cheyenne. Malcolm and Jane were posted to Seoul, Korea after leaving Niue and are now back in New Zealand. They now have two children. I have high hopes all of the above will visit before we're in wheelchairs.

Lisa lost her grandfather the year we left and she and her grandmother have sinced moved to New Zealand. Lower Hutt writes wonderful letters which keep us up on all the latest news; she also has another son. I hear from Olive once in awhile and Lofa Misa phones me. The Bushmans finished their term and are back in Nevada. Dr. Hussain is retired and back home in Pakistan.

The two years were very special, made so by the Niuean people. Some may wonder why I haven't written of the *important issues* of government and graft, of economy and ecology, and other lofty and complex subjects. These subjects are, however, covered in hundreds of books on hundreds of countries – nothing new, nothing different. No, others can handle these subjects with great expertise. I rather, was interested in the *people*.

These warm wonderful people opened their hearts and homes to us in such a way we were part of them. Others can write the dull technical facts. It is the individuals, the common people who prevail and we found the Niueans to be warm, kindly people. I doubt any of my Niuean friends have heard of St. Basil but they live by his words:

He who sows courtesy reaps friendship, and he who sows kindness gathers love.

Is it any wonder I say to myself this day – "I'd rather be shelling on Niue?!"